HOW TO
Talk To Your Cat

By
Lynn Allison

CONTENTS

INTRODUCTION

We humans use many methods to communicate how we think and feel to the rest of the world. We use body language, voice, gestures – even odor – as well as our language, verbal and written.

And in many ways, our non-verbal communication is more powerful than the words we speak and write. We raise our eyebrows to show that we are amused or curious or perplexed. We use our hands and our fingers to emphasize a thought or a statement. We smile and we frown, which tells the world we are happy or sad. We laugh and we cry to express feelings that are beyond the reach of our words alone. And an army of facial muscles mutely signals our otherwise most guarded emotions.

Roger Caras, who has written more than 50 books on animal behavior and communication, says:

"Humans communicate with each other in more ways than we realize. Our voices and deliberate hand signals are only a small part of it. Posture tells us a great deal even when we do not consciously evaluate what

> **"Cats are a mysterious kind of folk – there is more passing in their minds than we are aware of..."**
> – *Sir Walter Scott*

is going on around us. Odor is terribly important, particularly because it heightens our other senses. Odor can also act as a repellent or alienator. Eye-to-eye contact can be extremely important. A tiny touch can be electric. All of this transcends the spoken or written word."

What Caras is saying in this passage from his best-selling book, *A Cat Is Watching,* is that our body language – sometimes calculated, sometimes not – is often more meaningful to others than the words we speak.

For example, you can tell your husband that you love him, but if your teeth are gritted and that tension muscle in your jaw is dancing wildly, it's doubtful that he'll believe you for a minute!

It is this silent language that forms the basis of relationships with our fellow humans, and even more significantly, with our animals. Animals may not know the actual meanings of our spoken words, but they have an uncanny ability to read the language that our bodies speak – because they use the same skill in their own world. They "talk" to each other with body language, using every muscle, hair and expression in a vast, silent vocabulary to communicate their moods and feelings.

And so to establish a good relationship with our pets, we must learn to master our body language as well as understand theirs. This is especially true when it comes to communicating with your cats because they are particularly well equipped with a powerful understanding of body language.

PSYCHIC ABILITY

Many observers swear that cats, more than any other animal, possess a psychic ability that is positively uncanny. Cats throughout the ages have accurately predicted earthquakes and other disasters. They have even found missing persons.

They seem to know when danger, to themselves and to others, is imminent. They know when to stay or leave. They learn quickly who their friends are. They are fast reads.

There are stray cats living near my home that can actually tell time. A kind-hearted "Cat Lady" arrives at precisely six o'clock each evening to feed them. Minutes before she arrives, they assemble in a pack. They recognize her car and approach her, trustingly. Not one other person can get near them. She has established a lasting relationship with these cats due to her consistent, loving attention.

A colleague of mine, who shares her home with eight felines she rescued from the pound, actually does talk to her cats, and each one of them responds with loving sounds and gestures. Her cats guard her home, round up the gaggle of geese that circle the house, and delight visitors with their winning ways. These "trained" cats are striking proof that the attention and respect you give to your cats is returned in love and cooperation.

NO DUMB ANIMALS

Many people have successfully trained cats to do what most of us would dismiss as impossible if the proof were not so often presented before our very eyes.

Those remarkable cats that you see in television commercials have been lovingly persuaded by their owners to respond in the right kind of way to specific cues. They obey their masters not with the devoted dedication of dogs, but with the respect of one living creature for another.

It's not necessarily the words you use but the tone of your voice, your gestures and even your underlying mood that will make or break successful feline-human communication. Most animals are very sensitive to these kinds of signals. But cats, particularly sensitive to sound and more aware of the subtleties of body language than other domesticated pets, are extraordinarily attuned to these clues.

That's why successful cat owners work on their own communication skills, as well as the communication between themselves and their pets. If you send out signals of fear and uncertainty all the time, you better believe your cat will pay little attention to your commands!

And it is terribly important to be consistent and firm in your approach when communicating with your cat. These are very intelligent and perceptive animals. Cats know when you are happy or angry, and they certainly know when your command is worth a response or not.

People and cats have an incredible communication link, and many experts believe it stems from that uncanny ability to go beyond the obvious and concrete that both species share. Some call this ability a "sixth sense." The psychic researcher J. B. Rhine labeled it "extrasensory perception or ESP." However you define this mysterious but very real link that exists between humans and their pets, there are few cat owners who would deny that it exists.

I have shared my home with more than 20 cats over the years, most of them Siamese. Without exception, each one has had its own, very distinctive, personality.

"I have shared my home with more than 20 cats, most of them Siamese. Without exception each one has had its own, very distinctive, personality."

Bobby, my Sealpoint Siamese, is what you might reasonably call a "man" of few words. He'll look you straight in the eye and respond to any query with a single "Meow."

But my Brutus, a Bluepoint Siamese, talks non-stop when he wants something. He starts

11

before dawn with an often obnoxious tirade, and won't stop until he gets fresh food in his bowl and a romp outside.

Both cats, however, are similarly lovable. They enjoy nothing more than a good cuddle or a tummy rub. People who are not familiar with Siamese, and who assume that their reputation for a cold and lofty disdain is accurate, are surprised at how friendly and outgoing they are.

That is because loving communication can evoke the most positive response from your pet. Many people regard Siamese cats with suspicion, dismissing them as aloof and even hostile – remember those awful Siamese cats in the Walt Disney movie *Lady and the Tramp*? And certainly, some Siamese can be obnoxious.

For example, my sister's Siamese, Stanley, seems to go out of his way to intimidate visitors to his home. He snarls, bites, scratches and hisses with all the intensity and ferocity of a wildcat.

On a recent visit, Stanley came to the front door and adopted his customary aggressive stance. I could read the hostility in his piercing blue eyes! Enough is enough, I decided. I stood my ground, determination in every nuance of my own body language. I stared him down boldly and told him, mentally and verbally, that I would not put up with his behavior anymore. I didn't try to pet him or get him to come around. I didn't move until HE came to ME.

Are we now best friends? I can't say that. But certainly, on that day, he was smart enough to recognize what I was saying to him, and now we have a mutual respect for each other, if not a great fondness.

Another relative once had a particularly aggressive cat named Zorba. Zorba was extra-smart and a fast learner.

And he also developed a terrific understanding of human body language. When anyone with even a slight fear of cats visited, Zorba took particular pleasure in jumping all over his unfortunate victim, going straight into that well-practiced routine of aggression. I will never forget one particular aunt's reaction when Zorba jumped onto the couch behind her and bit her ear. My poor aunt almost hit the ceiling.

A few owners do think it's amusing when a cat exhibits antisocial behavior. But I don't recommend permitting aggression and hostility. With the right kind of attention, your cat will develop the type of personality traits that you want in him or her. Treat them with love and respect, and you will be rewarded with lovable, gentle behavior.

Author Carl Van Vechten put it succinctly in his book, *Tiger in the House:*

"A good-natured cat may be worried into becoming a bad-natured cat."

THE CAT'S MEOW

Many scientific experiments have proven what cat people have always instinctively known: Cats are perceptive – they can solve problems just like any other highly developed species.

Cats have been trained to turn things on and off. They can be trained to perform tricks, just like dogs. However, cats are stubborn by nature and require your best cognitive skills to get the best out of them.

Warren Eckstein, the author and animal expert, says of cat training:

"When you call a dog, he comes to you. But when you call a cat, he takes a message and gets back to you!"

One morning, my husband, who was in the kitchen, called Brutus. His ears twitched at the sound of his name. He lifted his pointed chin and uttered a "Meow!" Very negative.

The script progressed:

Husband: "Brutus! Come!"

Brutus: "Meow!"

Husband: "I SAID: Brutus! COME!"

Brutus: "Meow!"

With each response my husband's voice became louder and higher pitched. After the fourth, irate command, Brutus gracefully sauntered into the kitchen, leaped onto the table and began licking his master's face.

Now how do you chastise such a stubborn, but cute, cat? The answer is that you don't. What Brutus was doing was responding to the irritation in my husband's voice.

He was showing that he understood all right, but that he would come along only in his own good time.

Good communication with your cat not only serves as a means of training, but also of establishing a special, permanent relationship with your pet.

The internationally known animal trainer Gunther Gebel-Williams, who spent 42 years handling circus big cats, says that the more you talk to your cats, the closer you and they become. "Cats know if you are going to be nice to them by the tone of your voice, not the words that you speak."

He keeps Bengal and Siberian tigers as house pets, and still employs mutual respect – not the old-fashioned whip-and-chair method – to train his massive felines.

Beatrice Lydecker, in her book, *What the Animals Tell Me,* says that her work has demonstrated that you can't fool animals. "Cats, especially, have a finely-tuned sense of ESP, a non-verbal language that allows them to sort out situations in their minds long before we humans can.

"Like any true form of communication, learning how to communicate with your cat is a two-way street. It's give-and-take, command and listen. Once you have mastered the technique, life with your pet will be heavenly."

And Eckstein, who also embraces the concept of training cats with love, affection and ESP, says that if you firmly and truly believe that your cat is a part of the family and treat it as such, your kitty will respond.

For more about ESP, see Exercise and Your Cat.

"If you treat your cat with love, if you treat your cat with respect, if you treat your cat as if she is an intelligent, thinking animal, capable of making decisions, your cat will respond in astonishing ways."

FASCINATING FELINES

For thousands of years, the cat has aroused the curiosity, and the fascination, of humankind. In ancient Egypt, cats were adored to the point of worship, and killing a cat was punishable by death.

The Egyptians were the first people on record to document the establishment of domestic cats, bred from wildcats and imported to civilization along the Nile by the Ethiopians. With their mysterious airs and graceful movements, these cats were soon accorded the status of gods. Perhaps it was because they were creatures of the night, and the Egyptians were terrified of the dark. On a more practical note, they proved to be extremely useful companions. Cats kept rodents at bay, preserving crops and stored grain, and saving families from starvation and disease.

By 3000 B.C., 2,000 years after their introduction to the Egyptians, cats were revered members of the household. If a house caught fire, the cat was first to be saved! The Egyptian goddess of motherhood and fertility, Bastet, was depicted as having the body of a woman and the head of a cat. When a cat died, the head of the grieving family shaved off his eyebrows. The period of mourning did not end until his eyebrows grew back. And just like their human counterparts, dead cats were embalmed and buried in custom-designed coffins along with the necessary provisions – such as embalmed mice – to sustain them on their journey into the afterlife.

Cleopatra, as well as other wealthy ladies along the Nile, added liner around her eyes to give them a cat-like slant. Admired for her pest control value, worshiped for her mystique, envied for her fearlessness in the dark and emulated for her beauty, the cat thus enjoyed her absolutely finest hour.

But by the time the Dark Ages rolled around in Europe, things dramatically changed for the worse. Cats, identified by some obscure reasoning as the evil familiars of witches and suspected of being in league with Satan himself, became the target of religious wrath. They were ritually hanged along with the poor creatures who were condemned as witches. In pre-Elizabethan England, cruel archers even stuffed live cats and kittens into leather bags and used them for target practice.

Fortunately, cats found their way into the good graces of society again as the best thing then available to control the Black Death, a rat-borne bubonic plague, which swept through Europe with deadly frequency in the Middle Ages. Cats, once again, became valued members of society.

CAT FLAPS

By the 17th century, wealthy landowners in France built *chatieres* or cat flaps in the doors of their homes so that their pets could come and go as they pleased.

The first domestic cats to reach North America were a pair of fine ratters that a well-meaning French missionary gave as a gift to a chief of the Huron Indians. However, the Indians, who were not familiar with the peculiar skills and needs of felines, ignored the cats, and they eventually died without breeding. It wasn't until 1749 that cats were imported to the American colonies on the East coast from England to control the plague-carrying black rat.

But the intense affection and fascination that millions have today for these utterly absorbing pets is no new love affair. Great persons of the past such as Frederick the Great and Sir Winston Churchill adored their cats. Frederick, because of the superlative hunting skills of the cat, made them the official guards of the army stores and granaries.

Sir Winston Churchill's ginger-colored tomcat, Jack, slept with him on his bed every night and attended all the wartime Cabinet meetings at Churchill's elbow.

The prophet Mohammed so loved his cat that he permitted it to sleep within the flowing sleeves of his robes!

George Washington, Abraham Lincoln and the scientist Albert Einstein were all cat nuts.

The great tyrants of the world are recorded as being less than enthusiastic about cats. Alexander the Great, Napoleon and Hitler all heartily disliked cats. They led great armies, captured vast stretches of terrain and slaughtered millions of people, but they couldn't stand the mystery and the independence of the cat. No cat can be coerced, and perhaps that's what these dictators couldn't stand.

Today there are almost 60 million domestic cats in America, outnumbering dogs for the first time. All told, descended from the early Ethiopian cats first introduced to the Egyptians, there are now approximately 35 different breeds, all with their own enthusiastic followings.

For some cat fanciers, love borders on obsession. Cat owners spend $2.25 billion dollars each year on cat food. Billions more are spent on toys, accessories like litter boxes, litter and vet bills. You can have your pet freeze-dried and preserved for posterity after death. It costs $400 – and comes with a 20-year guarantee.

Why do we love cats? Clearly, it is an individual thing. Cats, experts say, reflect a shift in our sociological mood. While dogs are wonderfully loyal slaves, cats are the "thinking person's pet." As we grow to appreciate individuality in our own lives, we also learn to respect the independence of the cat. In other words, we admire in the cat those same qualities that we desire in ourselves.

There are, of course, more practical aspects, too. Cats are easier to care for, don't demand as much attention as dogs and generally get their own exercise. That's more and more important in families where both adults are at work most of the day, and for those who are too elderly or frail to walk a dog but still yearn for the companionship of a warm, fuzzy creature.

"CATSPEAK!"

Cat lovers often say their pet is so intelligent she can almost speak – and there are many ways a cat can say "Meow!" But she really talks to you with her body. A cat sees her owner as her mother, which is why a cat adores being stroked. A human hand stroking her fur feels just like the grooming of her real mother's tongue in kittenhood.

Watch how your cat runs to greet you with her tail held stiff and erect. This is how a little kitten will run to her real parent.

When you go into a room where your pet is napping, watch her open an eye, check out who it is, and then roll over on her back, exposing her underbelly. This is the ultimate compliment. It says "I trust you completely" – because in that position she is totally vulnerable.

That doesn't mean, however – as you may find out – that she wants that tender tummy stroked. It just means "I'm showing you how much I love you and how comfortable I am around you." Be flattered. You're doing a great job as a cat owner!

DISCIPLINE

If you need to discipline your cat, talk to her like a mother cat would. Suppose your pet isn't using the litter box. Grasp your pet gently by the scruff of the neck. The body will go limp and submissive – just as it did when her mother picked her up in kittenhood. Show your disapproval by growling...but softly.

The kneading owners are subjected to – sometimes painfully – when a cat jumps on their laps, begins purring loudly and seems to be sharpening her claws, is known as "milk-treading." The cat sees her owner settling down comfortably which is the same signal she received as a kitten from her mother when it was time to nurse.

DON'T GET MAD

What you should *never* do is get mad and push your pet away. Your cat will always be upset by this rebuff because no mama cat would push her baby away. This is a classic case of how interactions between humans and cats can be misunderstood.

Another classic of this kind is when a cat wags her tail. We often think it means our pet is angry. But that isn't so. It means she's feeling indecisive. For example, if a cat asks to go out, then realizes at the open door that it is pouring rain, she'll wag her tail because she's torn between wanting to go out and not wanting to get wet!

Cats also signal emotions by using their ears. There are five basic ear signals expressing relaxation, alertness, agitation, defensiveness and aggression.

Relaxed cat ears point forward and slightly outward, carefully listening to everything that is going on around her. When she stirs to investigate a noise, the ears go to alert – erect and facing forward.

An agitated cat usually twitches her ears nervously. A cat on the defensive flattens the ears tightly against the head – to protect them if a fight starts.

An aggressive – but not frightened – cat puts the ears at halfmast, halfway between the alert and defensive position. When she's like that, your pet is ready for any trouble that comes along.

THIS IS CAT LANGUAGE

To own a cat is to experience one of life's greatest mysteries – and challenges. There are those, of course, who will heartily disagree.

"I hate cats" is a not-uncommon cry from those who haven't experienced the glorious pleasure of feline company. Don't let your prejudices prevent you from beginning a relationship with a feline friend! You'll be delighted how rewarding, and fascinating, the experience can be if you honestly try to communicate with a cat and don't tend to regard it as simply a rather graceful ornament.

With their remarkable smarts, cats can provide their owners with both affection – and an ongoing intellectual challenge. Warren Eckstein, author and pet psychologist, says that cats are so intelligent that they simply won't hang around with a human being they don't like.

> **"At a touch, he explodes like a snapdragon into loud purrs..."**
> – Elizabeth J. Coatworth, *Portrait of a Young Cat*

"People don't choose or own cats," he says. "Cats choose the people they want to own..."

Those who are unaccustomed to cats may find what they see as aloof and detached behavior somewhat unsettling and uncomfortable. But with the right kind of unselfish communication and a healthy dose of love, you can develop a friendship that's utterly absorbing in its give and take.

When you learn how to talk to your cat, you can train her to come when you call, walk with you on a leash, do simple tricks, and even use a regular toilet as her potty if you want her to.

Cats are cuddly, too. There is nothing nicer than snuggling up to a contented, purring kitty at the end of a hard day. Cats – once they have been properly trained and socialized – have very little negative impact on a home.

If you and your cat have the right kind of relationship, there will be no "little accidents," furniture damage or any other kind of behavior that would upset even the most fastidious homeowner. And yet, although they are very independent, cats certainly do need your companionship and they do blossom when the lines of communication are established and strengthened with the human companion of their choosing.

And that is what this book is all about: teaching you, the owner, how to read your cat's moods and the signs she sends to you physically, so that you and she can become close friends and fast companions for life.

THE SIGNALS

Before we begin learning how to communicate with our cats, let's take a look at some of the ways they communicate with us – and each other.

Cats have a distinctive and consistent language that doesn't vary much from breed to breed, although some varieties of cats, like the Siamese, do tend to be more vocal. Whether you are blessed with a purebred, one of the rarer breeds, or you share your home with a stray that adopted you, you'll find these signals invaluable in helping you understand what your pet is saying to you.

PURRING

Purring is just one of the ways by which cats communicate. And although experts seem to be constantly debating all of the hows and whys of purring, any cat owner will tell you that it is definitely the sound of a contented kitty.

Here are some of the experts' theories:

"False" vocal cord: Cats possess vocal cords as well as another set of cords commonly called false vocal cords. When air is inhaled and exhaled, one false cord rubs against the other, thus creating that purring sound.

Muscle contraction: This theory says that some of the cat's laryngeal muscles contract in a special way and cause a buildup of pressure.

Turbulent blood: Turbulence is created when blood flow increases through the heart's main veins. It is most turbulent when the main vein constricts as the blood passes through the chest area. The swirling blood, say some researchers, creates a rushing, whirling sound, which is amplified by the diaphragm. Some experts say that after traveling up the air passages and into the head area, specifically the sinus and the skull, the noise becomes purring.

CATLORE

Although most cat lovers will insist that their kitties only purr when they are content, author Roger Caras says that the sound has little to do with happiness, pointing out that while purring actually begins when kittens are at the nursing stage, cats also purr while they are in some distress – when they are in labor, for instance.

"Cats purr when they are sick or even injured," he

says. "They purr when they are dying unless death comes suddenly and unexpectedly. Contentment just doesn't seem to do it. Profundity seems to be the key. When cats are profoundly anything – contented, in pain or any form of *extremis,* they seem to purr."

Desmond Morris, who wrote the milestone book, *The Naked Ape,* about the interrelationship of animal and human behavior, says in his recent book, *Catlore,* that he follows the false vocal cord theory because it is "... the most obvious and the simplest. Cats use their vocal cords for other kinds of noise," he reasons. "It's only obvious that they must use their false cords for purring."

Whatever is the true answer to this Great Purring Mystery, most of us cat owners do associate purring with contentment and take great pleasure in that comforting sound and the soothing vibrations we can feel when we fuss with our pets.

RAMBO & JOAN

Besides purring, cats have an enormous verbal vocabulary. Some, like my Bobby, are the strong silent types – a sort of Rambo with four paws and a tail.

Others are the Joan Rivers type – non-stop talkers who are adorable but can also be extremely trying. A good example is my Brutus, a real motor-mouth who can yowl for hours if I let him. Experts say that these individual differences are probably a mixture of individual genetics, specific breed and that most powerful influence, the mama cat.

After one exciting study that took place in 1944, researchers concluded that cats actually use nine consonants, five vowels, two dipthongs and one tripthong in their unique language! That's a lot of caterwauling there. If you then add to that the astonishing range and distinctive variations of pitch, volume and intensity, you soon realize that cats have a pretty broad working vocabulary.

Learning how to recognize the language and individual style of your own cat is absolutely essential to opening the doors of communication. The first thing you have to teach your cat is to establish free eye contact with you. Look directly into your pet's eyes and say something to her – such as a feeble "meow."

After a few attempts, you will discover that your pet will respond with an understanding "meow." Continue this exercise until you can maintain a conversation between the two of you from the opposite sides of a room.

Once you get the hang of this kind of kitty conversation, you will be able to elicit a whole repertoire of different sounds from your pet. We find that by changing our own intonation, we can get our cats to respond in kind, almost like an educated echo.

THE MEOW

As a general rule, meows can mean many things. They can be loud and demanding – complaints that dinner is late or that the door to the litter box room is closed. Meows can be short and sweet, an affectionate thank you for just being a friend.

Tiny mews are carry-overs from kittenhood. Cats use this very effective ploy to get what they want. Most of us cannot ignore the pitiful little mew that pleads for a treat or a simple fussing. It isn't all that unusual in human society, either. Women will use little-girl voices to get what they want from their men, men use little-boy pleadings when they want to be comforted.

THE YOWL

At the other end of this wide vocal range is that out-and-out yowl that grates on the ears and the nerves. It is a sound that gives a whole new meaning to the phrase "I want it now!" My Brutus is a true master of the yowl. He is generally very calm and quiet, but he launches into the most obnoxious tirade of yowls whenever he wants to go out – or in.

On Sunday mornings, when my husband and I look forward to a little peace and quiet from the workday world, this little monster proceeds to yowl us to distraction with his demands. Two minutes after letting him out of the house – to our enclosed patio – Brutus yowls to come back in. After awhile my usually patient husband, who acts as the cats' doorman, becomes irritable and yells in an attempt to quiet him.

At which point Brutus gives him a glare with his beautiful blue eyes and prances off to another room. This Sunday morning ploy has been going on for years. We don't know why Brutus gets a kick out of driving us crazy, but it is obvious he enjoys his Sunday morning scheme.

THE SCREECH!

This is a sound that pierces your very soul! If you have ever heard cats fighting, you will remember that high-pitched banshee wail that is calculated to scare off any opponent – as well as startle you awake, heart pounding, in the middle of the night.

If one cat doesn't retreat from the face-off, the caterwauling can go on for hours. It is an energizing, courage-mustering ploy that's similar to the yell of a karate expert as he delivers a blow.

HISSING

Hissing is another unmistakable sound. When you hear that, you know that your cat is telling you that she means business and that you'd better back off, at least for the time being. Hissing is the cat's way of letting the world know that trouble lies waiting. "I'm ready for trouble," it translates, "so you'd better not mess around!"

A few cat experts have suggested that this is the cat's way of imitating a snake, but most professionals really don't think that cats are into doing snake impressions! Hissing, more likely, is a cat's very own Defensive Early Warning System!

AND MORE...

There is a variety of in-between meows that you can learn to recognize if you study your cat's behavior. Remember that learning how to communicate with your cat begins with the simple but important act of observation. I can outline the signals that are generally associated with cat behavior, but you must learn to interpret what *your* cat is saying.

Listen closely to the sounds your cat makes. Get to know what she wants. Some cat owners try to imitate their pets' sounds so that they can establish a rapport through language. It's really not such a far-fetched idea once you get over your initial shyness. Try speaking kitty talk with your pet when the two of you are alone. Learn to mimic the sounds your pet makes and say them back. You'll be pleasantly surprised at how responsive your cat is just knowing you are making the effort to learn her language!

Roger Caras swears when he asks Kate, his lynx-point kitty, if she's a bad cat, she answer "Niao-ow!"

"And it's an 'n' sound, not an 'm' sound," he says. "Now I'm not going to insist that she knows the negative response, but she never responds that same way to any of my other questions."

IT'S IMPORTANT TO INTERJECT A LITTLE BIOLOGY HERE

One of the reasons why cats are so sensitive to sound is that they have an extremely acute sense of hearing. Their hearing range far outreaches that of the human ear, especially at the higher end of the sound scale. That's why cats respond to the higher pitch of a woman's voice more readily than they do to the lower register of a man. Men who want to communicate well with their cats really should try to cultivate a higher voice – no matter what their friends say.

Cats can pick up subtle nuances of sound we can't. This may explain why people have been in awe of what we regard as the cat's extrasensory advantage over us. Some experts swear that cats can identify members of a household by differing footsteps and movements, which doesn't surprise me at all. I've seen all my cats respond with a twist of their ears to unusual sounds, informing me that something is happening that I don't know about. It may be a plant falling in another room or a stranger approaching my gate. Cats make wonderful watch pets for this very reason.

And it is for this reason, too, that you should quickly learn to read your cat's signals, her sounds and her body language. They will give you important clues as to what your pet is thinking and how she will respond.

TELL-TAIL "TAILS"

I think the language of a cat's tail is beautiful. And that tail conveys a lot of information about how your cat is feeling.

I can spend hours, fascinated, watching my cats' tails. Their graceful movements remind me of the conductor of a world-famous orchestra directing a flowing symphony. The tail moves with a fluid grace and easy agility. It has purpose and dignity. Take a few moments and observe how your feline uses her tail to send you a message.

Waving tails can mean many things, such as the animal is confused or undecided about something. A wagging cat tail – unlike a dog's wagging tail – does not mean that the cat is friendly. In fact, it usually means just the opposite! Many a poor soul has been mauled because they mistook a cat's wagging tail as a sign of friendship.

Happy tails have no real display at all. They are neither stuck straight up in the air nor are they flopped down. The best way to describe them is as just there. An easy, relaxed air about the tail indicates that kitty is also relaxed and feeling pretty much at ease with the world around her.

Another happy tail is the one that usually greets cat owners when they return home after a day at work. The welcoming pet holds her tail directly vertical, straight up in the air from the rear end. With her tail in this position, your cat will also often display a quivering body motion, which indicates that she is happy and actually excited "all over" that you are home.

Aggressive tail signals are important to recognize. Many a cat owner has averted potential disaster by being an alert observer of tail tales. Warren Eckstein points out that angry tails have the same look about them as fearful tails, reflecting that fine line between fear and aggression. Cats, like most mammals including man himself, very quickly turn fear into fight, an instinctive tactic for self-preservation. Remember this always, and make sure to learn to communicate with your cat in a loving, non-threatening way. Cats will not tolerate attempts at intimidation, and their fear may prompt them to turn on the owner who tries to get obedience from his cat through dominance and bullying.

> *CAUTION!* **Beware of a swishing tail. The faster the swishing and the harder the thumping, the more dangerous is your cat's mood. Remember again that cats do not wag their tails with happiness the way dogs do. A mistake on your part may mean blood and tears, as well as hurt feelings!**

Bristling tails held in an upright, arched or curved position, says Eckstein, indicate trouble. And when a cat is truly frightened, the tail is not the only thing that will bristle. The hairs on her back will stand smartly to attention, as though she has been given an electric shock. This classic fright pose is seen time and time again in cartoons and comic books. It's funny when you see it there. But in real life, a scaredy-cat who displays this degree of fear should be definitely avoided. A scaredy-cat is a dangerous cat!

Submissive tails resemble aggressive tails. The thumping back and forth may mean that a cat has accepted your dominance. Look carefully to see if she's holding her tail a little low to the ground, certainly lower than usual. This may be your only clue that your cat is expressing submission rather than aggression.

Some cats will commonly adopt the most traditional and classic submissive pose: running from the scene with their tails tucked, literally, between their legs. And at the extreme end of submission, the cat curls up in a frightened little ball and may whimper or cringe. This is a very rare pose for independent cats and one that is usually the result of severe domination. It's bad from the point of view of cat and owner. If your cat has been

33

abused before you got her, it may take a lot of patience and work, and a lot of love, before you can start working with her as you wish. If you've had her as a kitten, and this pose is a result of your interaction, then you probably shouldn't be a cat owner at all.

Inquisitive tails are such fun to watch! Curious kitties will often conduct their fascinating treasure hunts, prancing around with their tails pointed straight up. Some cats add an enchanting little curlicue to the tip of their tails for good measure.

Balancing tails are just that. Cats use their tails to help distribute their weight properly when they find themselves in a precarious perch or situation.

Sick cats often hold their tails in one of the submissive positions. Very often, the more submissive the tail, the sicker the cat.

TAIL TIPS

Behavioral scientist and noted author Desmond Morris stresses these important tips for tail watchers:

- Each movement of a cat's tail sends out a signal that we, as humans, can decode.

- A tail that is slightly raised and softly curved indicates that the cat is becoming interested in something. When you are training your cat, you'll know if she is catching on by watching her tail react.

- A tail that is held very erect but with the tip tilted over shows that the cat is curious, but has certain reservations. She's somewhat puzzled.

- A tail that is fully erect, with the tip stiffly vertical, shows an intense greeting signal with no reservations. It's a delight to see in adult cats. It starts in kittenhood when it is the kitten's instinctive greeting to its mother.

- When the tail is held still but with the tip twitching, it means that the cat is mildly irritated. If the tip twitching becomes more pronounced – watch out! This cat is getting angry.

- When a female holds her tail over to one side, she's in heat. The tail held askew is a sexual invitation to the tomcat, who then knows he can mount her without fear of reprisal.

- When the tail is arched and bristled, the cat is firmly in a defensive mode and is preparing to respond to a threat or an attack. This, again, is a strong signal of potential danger. If the cat continues to feel provoked, an attack will follow.

THE EYES HAVE IT

To many pet experts, the eyes of a cat provide the most accurate picture of what is going on inside the mind.

Warren Eckstein again: "I truly believe that the eyes are the windows of the soul. Whether you are doing business over lunch and you need to assess the person sitting next to you, or whether you are dealing with ferocious lions, a gentle ape, or the cat in your home, close observation of the eyes can be a dead giveaway as to what's coming next."

Wide-open eyes mean that kitty is obviously awake and raring to go. If there is a glint in your cat's eyes, it means that she's also up to some mischief or another! That certain sparkle all cat owners have observed in their felines could also signal one of these amazing "crazy" moods. We've all known these to occur in our own pets, I'm sure. Suddenly, for no apparent reason, kitty will go scampering through the house at lightning speed, knocking over anything in her usually canny path.

I always know when Brutus is getting all geared up for one of his "crazies." His usually china-blue eyes somehow turn into blazing, reddened orbs, and he takes off like a greyhound out of the starting box, fairly flying up and down the stairs. It honestly seems as though his paws are barely touching the ground as he tears through the house!

Desmond Morris says these mad dashes are a classic example of what he calls "vacuum activity." Indoor cats, he explains, are generally deprived of an opportunity to express that innate ability to flee flat out from danger or hurtle at top speed after prey. And that is why, he says, they will suddenly "explode" into that frenetic burst of high voltage energy.

For first-time cat owners, it can be an unsettling experience – one lady I know who came to me for advice said that she thought her cat had had some kind of "turn" or was actually mentally unhinged! She was vastly relieved when I assured her that these seemingly insane rampages are perfectly normal for cats. Try to increase play time with kitty to help release some of this bottled-up energy.

DREAMLAND

Half-closed eyes mean that your pet is relaxed and ready to nap. If she is settled comfortably on your lap, you can be assured that in just a few minutes those eyes will close and she'll be in dreamland. But be aware that half-closed eyes can also indicate a problem. If your cat has half-closed eyes when she is wide awake, it may be a sign of an infection or illness, and you should take a closer look right away. Wait a day or so and, if it doesn't improve quickly, consult your veterinarian.

Closed eyes obviously mean that the time has already arrived for a nap. If your cat feels comfortable enough to nod off on your lap or close by you – feel honored. It means that she is absolutely comfortable in your company, and trusts you implicitly. You should be congratulated. You have been able to build up a terrific sense of trust and respect with your cat. Well done!

Snoring with closed eyes occurs only when cats are totally relaxed. This is yet another sign that your kitty loves you enough to let her guard down.

Dilated and enlarged pupils both indicate impending aggression. Do not approach when a cat's pupils are shut down, with mere slits showing – the body language says, "I'm ready for you!" Of course, a cat's pupils may contract in very bright sunlight, to control the amount of light the eye receives, and that's a different thing altogether. Use your common sense and good judgment to make sure of what your cat is saying through her eyes.

AND OTHERS...

A cat's mouth does more than meow. When kitty is relaxed, the mouth is also relaxed. The lips are in a normal position. However, an aggressive cat will display curled lips and an open-mouthed posture as part of the package designed to scare off any potential attacker. It is difficult to forget just how ominous a sight this is. A curled lip should always be taken seriously.

Whiskers on happy little kitties extend straight out and seem to reflect that inner contentment. Watch out for whiskers that are either pulled back tight along the face or bristling around the cheek area. This is a very clear indication that kitty is not a happy camper! They also can be a barometer for your cat's health. If the whiskers remain in an abnormal position for a prolonged period of time, check with your vet.

As I explained earlier in this book, your cat's ears are extremely sensitive and acutely attuned to a wide range of sound. They are also excellent barometers of your cat's mood. Many cat watchers look for "tell-tail" signs, and others search deep into the eyes to read their pet's moods. Personally speaking, I like to take a close look at my cats' ears.

Relaxed but alert ears will move calmly but determinedly around an area, gauging sound, direction and meaning.

Submissive or fearful ears are usually pulled back, lying flat against the head. They are in the perfect position to let others know that kitty is about to give in. During fights, cats often pull back their ears to avoid injury to these delicate and very important organs.

Aggressive ears are indicated by a slight rotation. The ear is in its normal position, but faces forward. The ears look like the wings of airplanes, ready for fight or flight.

Any emotional extreme will cause a cat's ears to twitch. This action indicates that a cat is very happy, frightened or aggressive, depending on the circumstance.

Cats that are sick will pull back their ears to show discomfort. If your cat's ears are persistently in the pulled-back posture, do consult your vet.

MORE SIGNALS

Cats love to stretch, yawn and roll over onto their backs for a pat and a cuddle. However, some cats simply adopt this posture for comfort. As said earlier, it doesn't always mean an invitation for play time. Many an eager cat lover has been the target of a feisty swat from a paw as a result of trying to rub a pet without checking for permission first!

Our cats simply adore tummy rubs and will roll over at, and on, our feet so that we cannot move without paying them some attention. I feel perfectly safe rubbing the tummies of cats I'm familiar with, but be aware that ALL cats will not respond kindly to having you touch that most vulnerable part of their body. Cats on their backs – like most other animals – are wide open to attack. It is a position in which they are most likely to be thinking defensively. So make sure that you have observed all the rules of body language and open communication before you touch a cat's tummy.

Cats adore rubbing up against things – especially you or your leg. Many cats actually rub their noses into yours to show affection. These acts of positive emotion are to be encouraged. There aren't enough friendly, loving cats out there, so do your best to tell kitty that you truly appreciate these warm gestures!

Licking is another way your cat expresses herself. Aside from the obvious principle of grooming with their tongues, cats can often tell you when there is something wrong. Constant licking in one area can mean kitty has a pain or a sore. Gently check the area, constantly reassuring your pet that you will deal with the problem kindly. Your tone of voice – soft but firm – will help your cat relax when you examine the affected area.

Sometimes cats will lick one area until it is entirely raw. This is known as a "hotspot" or granuloma. Experts say that such extreme licking is commonly rooted in a psychological problem – usually boredom. Put some bitter apple (available at pet stores or from your vet) on the area to discourage licking. Try to divert your pet's attention by playing games with her. Read the section, later in this book, on cats at play for some valuable tips on how to keep your cat's curiosity satisfied.

EARLY TRAINING

Learning how to communicate with your cat essentially involves a lot of sitting back and noting the signals she sends to you. It is only when you have learned how to "read" your cat's signals, and decipher what they mean, that you are ready to begin training your cat to respond to YOUR directives.

Be forewarned that training your cat means calling on your own reserves of patience and relaxation. Don't be in a hurry, for example, to get your kitty to sit. Don't try to rush your kitten into performing tricks. That just won't work. Cats are very independent and inherently stubborn. They will do what you want only after they decide to give you their full cooperation.

It's vitally important, of course, that you are very consistent in your training of your cat. She will pick up your slightest hesitation or ambivalence and decide from all of the signals that you give, your speech and your body language, whether or not you mean what you are saying.

And it is also vitally important to establish a very special, direct and unwavering eye contact with your cat when you are trying to send it a message.

THE RIGHT STUFF

There are skeptics who refuse to believe that cats can be trained. This is simply not true. Cats can perform most of the tricks dogs can perform.

They can sit, stay, come, fetch and heel on a lead. I've seen cats learn to perform the most incredible tricks – such as leaping onto their owners' shoulders or jumping through hoops on command. Cats, with that wonderful intelligence, perform an astonishing range of problem-solving skills – such as sorting out mazes and puzzles.

I've had cats who learned to walk on leashes better than many dogs. One of my cats, Chan, was such an excellent companion on his smart red leash that we walked many miles together. We had attracted a host of admirers on our meanderings. Most of the people we met were incredulous that a cat could become so well leash-trained. A few jokers, called out "Now, what kind of dog is that you have there?" The reality, of course, was that Chan loved human company and loved walking out on his leash.

If you would like to train your cat as a cheerful walking companion, you first have to exercise a whole lot of kindness, patience and positive reinforcement. This simply means giving your cat a lot of good vibes, and a lot of praise when she performs well.

First of all, invest in the proper equipment. Get a comfortable harness, or a cat collar that fits securely around the neck. It should be sufficiently loose-fitting so that it doesn't constrict the neck, but not so loose that your cat can escape with a tug and a determined wiggle of the head.

Select a leash that is comfortable for your height. If you can't find a cat leash that you like or that suits you – and there are plenty of leashes specially designed for cats – then one that is marketed for small dogs will do just as well. It should be lightweight, but well made. You don't want your kitty to break away! Check to make sure that the snap that attaches to the cat collar is sturdily constructed and clicks open and closes firmly.

When you bring the collar (or harness) and leash home, leave the items lying around for a while so that your cat will get used to them. Let her sniff them over and play with them, until her curiosity is thoroughly exhausted and the paraphernalia is accepted as just another part of the domestic scene.

COLLAR TRAINING

Once this is achieved, try gently laying the collar or harness on the cat's neck without actually putting it on. Do this, carefully and without fuss, several times a day. Many cats will shrug the collar off at first, so be patient. This kind of orientation takes time, perseverance and patience, but will be well worth the effort in the end.

Reward your cat each time you put the collar or harness on. Patting her on the tummy, or a special tasty treat – if weight gain is not a problem – is good behavioral reinforcement. Let your pet understand that putting on the collar or harness is a pleasant experience, not a negative one.

We all learn best by association, and cats are no different than the rest of us. Let kitty learn to associate the walking gear with happy, fussing times.

Now put on the collar or harness for brief periods of time, again rewarding your cat with a giant hug, a gentle scratch behind the ears, or whatever your feline likes best.

The next step is to attach the leash to the collar and then let your cat do whatever she wants to do. Let her roam through the house, dragging the leash behind her. Continue to do this periodically until kitty feels comfortable with both collar and leash and no longer fusses when you put them on her.

Now take your end of the leash and follow kitty around. Let your cat guide your footsteps. Don't force her to follow you, just play follow the leader until kitty is really comfortable with you on the other end of the leash.

After a week or so of this passive leash training, it is time to take the initiative and teach kitty to follow YOU. This is where all the communication skills you have ever mastered in your entire life come into play.

Use your voice, your body language, and a gentle, patient facial expression to get your cat to follow you. Use the high end of your voice range, the pitch to which your cat will be most responsive. Make your foray SOUND exciting and upbeat. For example: "Oh, boy, Susie! Are we going to have FUN! Come with me now and we'll have real FUN!"

Now, no self-respecting cat will follow you right off the bat. In fact, your voice will probably be rasping and your throat sore before a paw is moved in the direction you wish. Even then, the chances are that kitty will stop in her tracks, plant all four paws firmly in the rug and dare you to just try to make her move.

The worst thing you can do right now is get into a

fight for territory with your pet. The more you pull, the more resistance you'll meet. Use what I call the "popping" technique to give your pet a nudge in the required direction. Gently tug and release the leash, using a "popping" motion.

When you do this, repeatedly but gently "popping" that leash, your cat gets the message to move in your direction and that you are definitely not going to give in. Continue to encourage and praise kitty as you do this. Be gentle, but firm.

Warren Eckstein, who has trained many cats not only to walk on a leash but also to perform very difficult tricks for television commercials, advises getting down on your hands and knees and looking the cat directly in the eyes.

"Don't be disillusioned if your little furball moves only a few inches the first time," he says. "Keep at it. Soon you'll notice little breakthroughs. Just keep plugging away and kitty will eventually respond.

"Do not abuse this technique," he warns. "Don't yank the leash or become short-tempered and haul the cat in your direction. That gentle pull and release is all you need. Practice every day for just a few minutes daily. And if you become frustrated, do NOT take your feelings out on the cat. Punch a pillow or walk around the block by yourself!"

Now it is time to transfer your walks outdoors. If your pet has never been outside, take this step slowly and carefully. Kitty probably will be overwhelmed with the sights and sounds of the great outdoors. Take your pet on short walks, always praising her at every step.

After awhile, your pet will become much more at ease in the outdoors with you, and will actually nudge you to take her for a walk. Remember that this whole process takes time. Do not rush, or become angry or frustrated. If you lose your temper with your cat, you could lose any progress you've made.

COME, KITTY!

Just as dogs can be taught to come when they are called, so can your cat. The most important rule to remember is that you must be consistent and ready to follow through when you issue your command.

Both my cats come when either my husband or I call their names. Truthfully, we never really intended to teach them this "trick." Bobby and Brutus know that when we are calling them we have something pleasant in store. It could be a treat, a cuddle or simply to be let outdoors. Within seconds of calling their names, our two little furballs are at our feet – at least most of the time. As we have learned over the years, cats often take their own sweet time obeying a command.

Here's how you can train your cat to appear – almost always! – on command:

GET PERSONAL

- Use your cat's name when you call. Say, "Come, Rex. Come on!" Raise your voice slightly to achieve that higher pitch cats love.

- Make sure that you have a positive reinforcement to show to your cat when she comes. Don't use this command to administer medicine. Give kitty a pat or a treat when she arrives.

- During the initial training, it is helpful if you bring yourself down to your cat's eye level. This

45

approach helps build trust. If you are not the "giant" issuing commands, your cat will be more responsive.

❧ Each and every time your cat comes to you, issue profuse praise. Cats love to be stroked and patted. Use this positive reinforcement cue to build a solid foundation for training.

❧ If your cat doesn't come when you call, do not chastise or punish. Simply ignore your pet until your wishes are responded to positively. Make sure that every member of the family follows suit. It's no use training your cat to come when called if someone else gives in and gives the cat a reward for not obeying the command.

❧ Limit your training sessions to several minutes daily. Cats do not have a long attention span and will simply not stay involved long enough for a lengthy training session to be of any value. You are best off staggering your efforts into two or three mini-sessions of five minutes each per day.

❧ If your cat is particularly obstinate and moseys over several minutes after you issue the "come" command, praise her anyway. Eventually she'll get the message.

WARNING: Do not practice this trick outdoors if kitty is off the leash. Cats may pick up a scent and run after prey instead of obeying your command. Don't take a chance that your cat may run off and risk the tragedy of an accident.

SIT!

I've never attempted to teach my cats this trick simply because, for me, it doesn't contribute much to my relationship with my cats. It's more important that my 80-pound Labrador dog sits on command, before he leaps, all muddy paws, onto my guests.

However, my sister's cat, Stanley, routinely sits upon command. He also takes part in a game they both enjoy – pointing to her closed fist with his paw, and guessing which hand holds his treat!

First of all, kneel alongside your cat, turning your face toward her. Using the hand closest to her neck, place one or two fingers under her collar or harness.

Now place the other hand under her tush at the "knee joint" and gently tuck in the rear, adjusting her body into a sitting posture.

At the same time – but very gently – lift the collar slightly upward. Say "sit" as you perform these two moves simultaneously. Make extra sure that you do not jerk or frighten kitty. Smoothly push the rear-end down and under while pulling the collar upward. This motion helps your cat understand what is required, and the general direction in which you want the movement to take place.

When you say "sit," emphasize the "t." This gives your kitty a firm handle on this special command word. Don't use your pet's name at the same time as you use this command. This may confuse or excite the cat into jumping up rather than sitting still. Instead, keep the training sessions limited to the "sit" command. Speak gently and softly and do not become upset if your pet refuses to perform. Try again later on. And don't forget to be fulsome in your praise, when kitty gets it right! Your little student loves to know that she's done well.

47

STAY, KITTY!

I think of this command as very, very important. To me, it could well mean the difference between life and death for my pets. Every beloved pet should be taught this command if at all possible.

It is a response – I cannot call it a trick – that may save their lives from an oncoming car or any other kind of potential threat. It's also most useful during grooming, when you want your cat to remain perfectly still while brushing her fur or clipping her claws. It's also handy when you take your cat to the vet for an examination or when guests are arriving and you don't want your precious pet to dash out through the open door.

With all four of my pets, I practice the "Stay!" command daily, to reinforce it as insurance against disaster.

By the way, just like any other form of training, you should reinforce any trick or command you teach on a daily basis. Once a week is simply not enough.

Enough said.

In order to get kitty to stay, put on your most confident voice and practice your body language in the mirror. Do you recall, at the beginning of the book, that I emphasized the importance of body language in pet communication? Well, no other command works better than "Stay!" when it is accompanied by a clearly positive body signal as well as a firm voice. YOU are in authority here, and that cat will STAY!

That is the message you want to get across to kitty. With this command, unlike sit or come, there is no room for wavering or error. Out in the real world, fraught with danger, there may not be a second chance.

This is where diligent and consistent training pays off. If you let kitty know that you are unsure of yourself during training, she will pick up your signals and simply not respond. But if you clearly demonstrate who is the boss – especially with this "Stay!" command – you will get results.

Keep in mind, however, that even if you are super-firm and consistent with this command, your pet will probably not learn this command overnight. It could very well take weeks and weeks of patient effort, but you will discover it will be well worth all that time and energy in the long run.

Control is crucial when you begin to use this command. So it is better if you have already taught your cat to be

at ease and happy in a collar or a harness. Place two fingers under the collar and hold the cat firmly while issuing the "Stay!" command. Warren Eckstein advises reinforcing the verbal command with the traditional hand signal for stay, which is placing your palm toward the cat's face, fingers pointing downward.

Repeat the command as you hold the cat firmly in place. After awhile, let go of the collar or harness and look your cat straight in the eye and repeat the "Stay!" Remember, do not use your cat's name when you issue this command. That will confuse your pet, making her think that you want her to come to you.

Eckstein offers a piece of advice:

"When you issue the 'Stay' command, prolong the word to give your pet the verbal idea that this is special," he says. "Say, S-t-a-a-y... so that kitty knows she is not to move."

It is very important to keep remembering that the secret to success in training is to repeat the performance as often as possible and in a very positive way. It is not necessary for your pet to remain frozen to the one spot, like some concrete statue, but it is important that she remains in the same general area until you say it is okay to move.

You may want to pick out a specific spot near the entrance to your home as the training area. This is a very practical thing to do because working here will specifically help to avoid that pet owner's nightmare – the potentially disastrous Great Escape when guests are arriving, or when the door is accidentally left open.

Plop your pet down in the spot and issue the "Stay" command. When she tries to move out of the area you have mentally and physically designated for her, give your kitty a firm "No."

Remember that your cat has a quite uncanny perception of your mental powers, so use mind signals – or telepathy – as well as these verbal and hand signals to make your cat follow your instructions. Don't laugh! I promise you that this works! Cats may not be able to read minds in the classic sense, but they can interpret what you are thinking and decode it for themselves. If you are mentally tough when you issue the "Stay!" command, you will certainly help reinforce your message.

GOOD KITTY!

Don't forget to lavish praise and hugs on your pet during these training sessions. Cats – just as much as dogs – love to be scratched, petted and cuddled. Praising your cat for a job well done with lots of hugs and cuddles is far, far better than snack treats.

That's true for two reasons. The first, most obvious, is that too many treats for cats — just like humans — means a bulging waistline and a threat to good health.

The second is that you may need to issue a command to save your pet's life at a crucial moment. There won't be any treat on hand to tempt her to obey then!

My brother, Peter, is very adept at cat training. He trained three of his most recent cats to go potty on the human toilet. The way he does this is with a special device (available at your pet store) that fits on top of the toilet seat.

HERE IS THE METHOD HE USES

He brings the standard cat litter box closer and closer to the toilet each day until the cat feels comfortable doing her business next to the toilet.

Then he elevates the litter box so that it sits on the toilet seat. After a week or so, the cat will feel perfectly at ease going to the bathroom in the elevated litter box. After that, he transfers the litter into that special device from the pet store that fits right over the opening of the toilet. The cat now learns how to balance herself on the seat and "aim" into the center of the toilet. After another week or so, he removes the litter holder and the cat uses the toilet just like you or I.

Now if he could only learn how to train his cats to FLUSH the toilet after use, we'd have a truly purr-fect situation!

SHOWBIZ

Cat trainers whose pets are in show business spend a remarkable amount of time painstakingly training their pets to perform a whole range of tricks. A gorgeous snow-white Persian that you have seen on TV in Purina commercials – her real name is S.H. III, after her owner Scott Hart of California – has an amazing repertoire of tricks. Scott, her owner, is low-key about her skills.

"Oh, she's just a very smart cat," he says, "...and she's always eager to please me."

But, his modesty aside, he has obviously worked very hard at developing a trusting relationship with his cat, the firm basis for pet training in general.

LET'S GO OVER THE RULES ONE MORE TIME.

1. By observing, learn to understand what your cat is saying in different situations. Learn to read cat body language. Learn to decipher the various noises and sounds your cat makes. And, most important of all, learn how to recognize when your pet is relaxed, tense or frightened. There is absolutely no use at all in trying to train a frightened, unreceptive feline.

2. Be calm and patient. Rome wasn't built in a day and cats most certainly won't be trained in a flick of their tails. Don't lock yourself into a timetable. Be flexible. So if it takes your kitty another week or so to learn how to sit, who cares? You've got many years ahead of you to enjoy with this animal.

3. Use a special voice to train your pet. Remem-

ber that cats have a greater hearing range for higher sounds, so talk to your cat using the high end of your voice range. Make your voice sweet but firm. Emphasize the command words by drawing out the vowels and attacking the consonants. Use kitty's name only when you are issuing the "Come!" command.

4. Reward with praise, not treats. And reward each and every good performance. A simple pet, a scratch behind the ears or even a gentle kiss on the nose is fine. (Yes, cats do love kisses!)

5. Repeat, repeat, repeat! It is difficult to overemphasize the importance of repetition in training, and it is crucial not only during the initial training period itself, but also in the daily reinforcement of the work afterward. You must keep the commands fresh in your kitty's mind.

You want to have your cat – like any pet – so conditioned to respond to your command that it will react automatically, almost without thinking. But you must remember too, that cats are very intelligent and finicky pets who might fool you just when you think you've got a certain command down pat. And it's really never a simple memory lapse on kitty's part.

It's simply her way of letting you know who is really the boss!

HEALTHY AND HAPPY

A healthy cat is a vital and playful fellow who adores a good game not only for sport, but also for the very important exercise it provides.

Since most of us have indoor cats, they simply do not get enough natural exercise to keep them fit. That's why obesity is such a real problem in many of our cats.

Fat cats simply are not desirable, no matter how adorable they may be to watch. If you allow your cat to become obese, you are doing her a great disservice. You are asking for a multitude of health problems as well as shortening her life.

In order to keep kitty's weight under control, you should do two things: Watch her diet and increase her exercise. Just as with humans, this double-pronged approach is the safest and best way to keep your pet's waistline trim.

Another plus of regular exercise is that it helps prevent, and can even cure, certain behavioral problems that we will discuss shortly. A well-exercised cat gets into less mischief than an under-exercised cat, which may become neurotic and go looking for trouble.

"When I play with my cat, who knows if I am not a pastime to her more than she is to me?"
– *Montaigne*

You can exercise your cat by making simple little toys, such as a ball of wool suspended on a string that is attached to a door knob. We'll tell you more about this fascinating sport of tetherball in the next chapter.

Do provide a variety of toys for your cat, including some catnip toys that, as you probably know already if you are a cat owner, will make your pet particularly frisky. Siamese cats, I have found, seem to be immune to the giddy effects of catnip, so don't be surprised if your Siamese isn't the slightest bit impressed by that special catnip present!

Spend time tossing toys around the room, allowing your cat to chase them willy-nilly and bring them back to you if you both enjoy that. This is both a game and a trick you may want to add to your repertoire. Fetch is an easy trick to teach. Cats are such natural show-offs. They like to bring their "prize prey" back to Mom or Dad to show how well they've done on the hunt.

My first Siamese, Chan, would present me with the remains of rabbits and mice with awful regularity each morning when we lived in the country. He never actually ate his hapless victims. We didn't keep him hungry, so he didn't kill for food. He just followed these deadly instincts of his and headed off on a hunt at dawn each day to ply his trade.

Pound for pound, zoologists will tell you, our domestic cats are the most deadly hunters in the entire animal kingdom. On one memorable occasion, Chan came home with a snake dangling out of his mouth! In all fairness, despite my squeamishness, I had to praise Chan for a job well done, although I was mightily disgusted by it all!

Pounce games are great fun for your feline. Hide an object under a sheet of newspaper and let kitty pounce on the "hidden prey." To make the game even more interesting, tie a piece of string to the object and make it move around under the paper. Oh my, your kitty will love that!

For more cat games, turn to page 63.

CURIOUS

Cats are insatiably curious. They will stop at nothing to investigate whatever intrigues them. Open drawers are excellent opportunities for feline fantasies. Leave your dresser drawers open about six inches and watch kitty climb in and out of the drawers, inspecting the contents very officiously. We have given the nickname The Inspector to one of our cats, Bobby, because of this passion of his. He has an absolutely uncanny ability to dart into any open drawer, cupboard or through a door that is open barely a crack, in a split second. Of course the down side to this game is that if you forget that kitty is in your dresser drawer, you can close him in.

Bobby doesn't let us forget about him for long, although on one occasion The Inspector dove into my husband's dresser as he was preparing to leave for work. We came home hours later and heard a plaintive "meow" coming from the bedroom. Sure enough, there was Bobby, huddled, somewhat unhappily, among the sweaters!

Cats also love to tinker with pens, pencils or other easily moveable objects. They use their graceful paws to bat small objects left lying on a tabletop. They seem to take great delight in knocking these things onto the floor. Great fun for kitty but a little irritating for pet owners!

TWOFERS?

There is an excellent case to be made for having more than one cat – for me, two is the perfect number. Having a partner not only makes for great companion-

56

ship but also helps in the exercise routine.

Cats will play with each other spontaneously when the energy level demands it – or the weather changes suddenly – without any involvement on the part of us humans.

If you do introduce a new pet into your household, make sure it is a kitten. It's much easier to bring a baby into the house when you have an older cat, although I can think of many cat owners who have successfully introduced adult cats into the home with little or no fuss.

If you decide to bring home a companion for kitty, make sure the newcomer has had all shots and is flea-free. At first, isolate the new cat in a separate room or cage with her own food, water and litter. Let the older cat get to know and feel comfortable with the newcomer. After a day or so, let the new cat out to play in a supervised atmosphere. Chances are your first cat will hiss and try to attack the new cat. Tell her firmly, "No!"

After two or three days, your first cat should feel much less threatened and may even be curious about the new kitten. In this case, feel free to let the newcomer out of her secluded area to play with your first cat. Nature works in wondrous ways and I have seldom seen two cats not get along if they are brought together gradually and encouraged with love. Remember that this book is about communication with your cat and how to get your message across to your cat. By being positive, you can let your cat know what you expect – and that is good, sociable behavior.

FEEDING YOUR CAT

Let your veterinarian be the judge of what kind of food is best for your cat. In general, the premium brands that are sold in pet stores and through your vet are by far the best.

These brands, also called professional or alternative foods, have much more nutrition than supermarket brands. In a recent study of cat foods, a whopping 85 percent failed to meet National Research Council (NRC) standards for the minimum levels of essential nutrients! Another 50 percent failed to provide what their own labels promised!

It is definitely worth the extra few cents to buy your cat the best available food. In the long run you will have a healthier pet, and a well-nourished, healthy cat will save on the vet bills.

There are four basic kinds of cat food: canned, semi-moist, dry and homemade. Ask your veterinarian to prescribe the proper menu for your cat's individual needs. Most experts agree that a mixture of dry and canned food at alternate meals is the best formula.

Canned food is higher in fat but is more palatable than dry, making it an excellent choice for the most finicky kitty. Also, for cats with urinary problems – a condition that affects most neutered males – canned food is better because of its higher water content. From a storage point of view, of course, canned food does have a higher shelf life than dry or semi-moist.

Semi-moist comes in easy-to-open pouches that are also easy to store. It doesn't spoil if left out, as canned food does, and generally contains more nutrients than canned food.

Semi-moist food has its disadvantages, however. These

foods often contain coloring agents that may be carcinogenic. It is also generally more expensive than the equivalent measure in canned foods.

Dry food is low in moisture and has a high concentration of nutrients. It's much cheaper than canned food and doesn't require refrigeration. It can be left out all day, which is an advantage for pet owners who prefer to "free-feed" their cats instead of filling their dishes only at regularly scheduled mealtimes.

Dry food helps promote dental health because it removes the tartar on a cat's teeth. And it also has more vitamins and minerals than canned or semi-moist food. The disadvantages are that dry food contains preservatives which can pose health problems for allergy-prone cats. They are also high in microorganisms (molds, insects and fungi) which promote disease. Some cats simply do not like the taste of dry food and others cannot digest the high-fiber content.

With the exception of a few specialized brands – the label will tell you which – most dry cat foods are very high in minerals, especially magnesium and salt, which in some cats may lead to urinary tract infections.

HOMEMADE

Homemade foods can be purchased through mail order and specialty stores. Several supermarket chains do carry these in a flash-frozen form. Check with your health food stores and local animal feed stores if you are interested in these lines.

The main advantage of homemade cat food is that the ingredients are fresh and the nutrients are professionally balanced. The main disadvantage, of course, is price. But if you have a show-quality cat or simply wish the best for your pet, this may be the way to go – or, of course, you can always do the cooking yourself.

Experts do not advise owners to simply use "people" food or recipes for their cats. If you insist on preparing your own meals, please ask your vet for specially designed recipes that meet all your cat's requirements.

Here's a quick, ideal content guide:

🐾 Protein – 35 percent

🐾 Fat – at least 15 percent

🐾 Ash – no more than 8 percent

🐾 Moisture – no more than 15 percent

In canned foods, the water content can go as high as 70 percent, and the protein as low as 12 percent.

In addition to serving kitty the best possible diet to ensure good health, you may want to add a vitamin supplement of some kind. Some cats thrive on a teaspoonful of olive oil each week or two to help ease the expulsion of hairballs. Always check with your vet before adding or subtracting foods or nutrients from your pet's diet.

Make sure that fresh water is always available for your cat. If you live in a warm climate, put an ice cube or two in the dish to keep it palatably cool.

THESE SHOTS!

No animal can be expected to be cooperative and trainable unless it is healthy. It is very important to have your cat checked by your veterinarian on a regular basis.

And the best way, I've found, to find a good vet is by asking other pet owners whom they recommend.

Cats and kittens need protection. It is crucially important to make sure that your cat or cats receive the recommended vaccinations at the optimum time. If you adopt an adult cat, find out if you can, when she was given her last shot.

In general, a kitten will receive between two to four vaccinations, depending on your vet's recommendation. The actual number varies depending on the kitten's age at the first visit, whether the mother was vaccinated, and whether or not the kitten may have been exposed to another sick animal.

The first vaccination is usually given at around six to eight weeks and other vaccinations are given at four-week intervals after that until the kitten is twelve to sixteen weeks old. The program should give your pet protection against distemper (feline panleukopenia), rabies and respiratory viruses. Many vets now also recommend vaccination against feline leukemia.

Vaccines work by activating the body's immune system. Each shot produces a carefully modified form of the actual disease it is designed to protect against. When these agents – called antigens – are introduced into your cat's body, they are recognized as foreign substances by the immune system, which produces antibodies to combat them.

If, subsequently, your cat is exposed to one of these potential killers, the antibodies will beat it and prevent serious harm or death.

Remember that even housebound cats can be exposed to a wide variety of viruses. They can be airborne or easily brought indoors by you or guests – on clothing, for example. Remember that timing is most important. Have your pet inoculated at the earliest recommended time, right away if your cat is an adult. And as she gets older, make sure to get the appropriate booster shots.

CHECK DAILY

Keep a watchful eye on your pet. It's important to look your cat over daily with health in mind. When you're petting or stroking, be on the alert for injury, parasites, unusual bumps or lumps. Cats are prone to tumors and early detection can be the difference between life or death.

Keep an eye on stools. If diarrhea lasts for more than a day, try to determine which cat has a tummy-ache. Curtail feedings for a while and offer the sick cat plenty of water to prevent dehydration.

Very often, by really communicating with your cat, you will automatically know when she isn't feeling well. Check her nose daily to make sure it is cool and moist. Smell the ears and check the eyes for unusual discharge, which may signal infection.

A daily health check will go a long way to prevent major problems. Your loving attention to your precious pet says that you care.

EXERCISE AND YOUR CAT

You don't have to invest in fancy equipment to keep your cat in good shape. There are all kinds of great low-cost – or no-cost – games to keep Puss alert and active.

Although the best exercise for an indoor cat is playing with another cat, your single housebound pal can still enjoy many hours of fun and exercise. Best of all, many of these games, described in *Cathletics* (Castle) by Jo and Paul Loeb, will be a blast for you, too.

NOTE THESE GUIDELINES:

1. The game is its own reward. Don't give a treat or praise for playing.

2. Your cat has tremendous hunting instincts and an incredible sense of hearing. Use them to your advantage in these and any other games.

3. Don't FORCE your cat to play with you. If you make the game look fun, her natural curiosity will bring her over. In fact, once she knows what's involved, she'll often invite YOU to play!

4. Make a point to touch and handle your cat. Physical contact is a must in cat play.

5. Neither you nor your cat can win all the time. Just as in hunting, the fun is in the challenge.

6. We all know there are different strokes for different folks, and the same goes for cats. Take some time to figure out what turns your cat on. Let her show you what she wants to play and how she likes to do it. Take a game she enjoys and change it around. Most of all, do things she likes – again and again.

7. Don't forget – these games are meant to be fun. If one of you is forcing the other to do something you don't want, think it through again. Have a good time!

GAMES FOR PUSS TO PLAY ALONE

The Stair Game: Here's a nice variation on "fetch" that features what amounts to a game of automatic ball return.

Mitzi, a long-haired, white-nosed black female, lives in a house with a finished basement. Stairs lead up to the kitchen. Mitzi has learned to bring a silver ball to the top step, then drop it, and watch it bounce down the basement stairs. When it's halfway down, she gives chase, and finally corners her metallic prey in a far corner of the basement. Then she brings the ball back upstairs and the game goes into another round.

Here's how to get your cat started. Stand at the top of the stairs. After your cat comes to see what's going on, drop a ball and let it bounce down the stairs. When she sees what it is, she'll run down to chase after it.

At least at first, she probably won't bring it back up. If you want to exercise yourself as well as your cat, you can go get the ball for her, run back up the stairs, and roll it down again. Otherwise, take a series of objects with you. This way, you can just sit up there and throw them down until she tires of the game.

Tetherball: This is an ideal solitaire game that was created for Little Cat, a white and yellow fluffball. His owners tied a hollow plastic ball to the closet door knob by a long piece of twine. Little Cat stalks the ball and thwacks it with his paw. This makes it swing through the air, usually making a satisfying clack against the wooden door of the closet. Little Cat's paws keep it in motion, but the string keeps it captive and prevents it from rolling off to where he can't get at it. And its arcs and loops encourage him to leap and stretch – and keep playing longer.

GAMES TO PLAY TOGETHER

Bubble Chasing: Bubbles hold a cat's attention for hours because they can't be caught. And the way they constantly move, change shape and adjust color attracts any cat's attention.

Buy a jar of bubble solution for kids. You can also make your own with a good soap base. For giant bubbles, add a few drops of glycerin. Dip in the little plastic wand that comes with the jar. Make bubbles either by blowing through the wand or wafting it in the air. Your cat will be fascinated by the bubbles, and it won't be long before she's batting away at them with her paws.

Don't always blow in the same direction. Keep your cat moving. She won't be able to believe she never gets anything with those quick swipes, and her determination will keep her going.

Stalking the Wild Feather Duster: One secretary finds she can give her cat, Whiskers, some good exercise with one of those feather dusters that are so convenient for getting into hard-to-reach places. She waves this duster in front of Whiskers, and he jumps for it. When she tickles him with it, Whiskers rolls over, scratching at the feathers with his paw. Even if not actually offered the duster, he will try to grab for it – sometimes leaping high up in the air. Once again, to keep your cat interested, you've got to keep the duster active.

Shadows in the Night: This is a perfect evening game. Get hold of a strong flashlight or slide projector. Turn off the lights. Flash the light on a blank wall and prop up the light source so that your hands are free.

Now play shadow games like you did when you were a child, making rabbits, chickens, snakes and any other creatures you can. Be aware: Any object you hang in front of the light will cast its magnified shadow on the wall, but huge shadows may make a scaredy-cat run away. Play with her by making the shadows approach and retreat. If she's right next to the wall, the smaller, "bite size" shadows will attract Puss's attention. Soon she'll be leaping up at the wall, trying to catch hold of the elusive shapes.

Pawball: Here's a good late-night bedtime game. A cat tends to wake up at night, so a little pre-bed exercise will tire her out enough to help her doze – and let you sleep. Your only equipment for this game is a plastic "knotball."

❧ *How to Make a Knotball:* Get a plastic bag from the cleaners, one of those sheaths the paper comes in, or a clean plastic grocery bag. Stretch the plastic into a rope, then tie a knot, and then another. Soon, all those knots in one place will form a wad of plastic about an inch thick. Then take a sharp scissors and clip off the remaining plastic on each end.

This knotball will travel across the rug at good speed, but better still, it responds to the pressure of your cat's jaws and claws. It's a lot squishier than an aluminum ball, which could hurt your cat. And the more she chews it, the softer it will become.

Toss your knotball up over the bed and let it bounce off the wall. Your cat will jump up, trying to catch it in midair. She will either bat it with one paw or grasp it between both paws and carry it to her mouth. Some cats will bat it back and forth on the bed for a few minutes. Then they will let you have it back when they want you to start the game over.

Don't let your cat catch the ball every time. Sometimes grab it yourself before she can reach it. Pretend to hide the ball from her, and then bring it out from nowhere. Pretending to toss it a couple of times before actually doing so will really get her excited. Use "corner shots" that bounce off the ceiling and "drop shots" that hit high on the wall and fall nearly straight down. Go to the foot of the bed and throw a low line drive over your cat's head – a shot that's easy for her to intercept. Remember, the ball is "in play" only as long as it remains on the bed.

Weightless Wheelbarrow: Remember playing wheelbarrow as a kid? In that game, the fun was holding vertical people horizontally. Since your cat already walks on all fours, the trick here is to make her vertical – by having her literally climbing the walls.

Cradle the lower part of her back and hold her sideways so her front paws rest against the wall. When she goes to "walk" forward, let her – as if her hindquarters were being dragged along automatically.

Being wheeled on walls makes a cat feel that she's a

real daredevil. It also gives her a chance to check out the picture frames, thermostats, etc. Hold her securely under her hips and shoulders and she can even walk on the ceiling. Be sure to always press her closely enough to the wall so she can walk without slipping.

Snap the Cat: Have you ever watched kittens tug each other around, especially on a slanted or slippery surface? You can give your adult cat the same thrill. If you have a room with a linoleum or hardwood floor, seat Kitty on a scrap of carpet or an old but clean dishtowel and tug her around. You can also teach her to dig in her claws and let herself be dragged across the floor. If she likes roughhousing, you can let her slide some distance on her own. Try to arrange things so she lands in a soft cushion, preferably stuffed with goose down.

If your room is carpeted, a low cardboard box can make a great "sled." If you don't want to bend down that far, a rope or tether works just as well. Soon your cat will go over to her towel or box and meow, waiting for you to pull her. Just don't pull so quickly, or so hard, that your cat is jerked off her feet!

The Shell Game: This is just what it sounds like – the standard shell game done in bars and on street corners. When it comes to playing with your cat, however, this is no sucker's game. Cats have such keen sight that they have no problem following that one shell with the pea underneath it.

Take three identical "shells" – small bowls, opaque paper cups, plastic shaving cream can lids, empty cat food cans, or any other small, easily moveable containers. Sit your cat on the floor or table in front of you and start pushing two of the shells around. Get her attention by asking her "What's that?"

Let her see and smell the interior of the two shells. Then show her what she's "betting" on. You can use a food reward. Either hide a piece of dry food under one shell, or quickly give one to your cat as soon as she locates the pea. Some cats will even play if you put a favorite toy underneath the "shell."

Wiggle the object around in your fingers. Crunch it against the floor so it makes noises. Pretend it is exotic and mysterious and possibly unattainable. Switch it from hand to hand. Hide it, then bring it out. Throw it in the air and catch it. If you play with it, she'll want to try it herself.

Once she's really paying attention, hide it under one of the "shells." Switch them around. After you stop, pick up the shell with the object underneath it (that is, if you still know). Give her the treat, or let her play briefly with the toy. Do it again, but this time, wait and see if she'll go for the "shell" with the object under it, either by nosing or pawing at it.

Once she gets the idea and is getting pretty good, go to three shells. Sometimes she'll win, sometimes she'll lose. But as long as you keep up the action and make it interesting, she'll keep playing.

Telepathy: For the advanced cat/human team, try sending psychic messages. A cat owner named Matt swears his pal Amos comes to him far faster when he summons him telepathically than when he calls him out loud!

❖ If telepathy works for you, it promises a whole new closeness between you and your cat. The only secret is to imagine the cat doing just what you want her to – then wipe the image from your mind. A successful "hit" will register almost immediately.

MENTAL HEALTH

Neurotic pets? It can happen to anyone. Some pets turn phobic (develop deep-seated fears that put them into a panic), some regress to infantile behaviors (kittenish behaviors that are inappropriate for them at their age), some become hypochondriacs, while others – like the toy poodle who took on the mastiff – may develop delusions of grandeur.

Surprise, surprise: Often the neuroses start with their owners, who unknowingly encourage the odd behavior in their sensitive pets. But no matter how it starts, extreme behavior problems need to be nipped in the bud for the comfort and mental health of all concerned, whether they walk on two legs or four.

Daniel Tortora, Ph.D., is an animal psychologist and author of *Help! This Animal Is Driving Me Crazy*. He's dealt with many bizarre cases of animal behavior, including one where a small dog had actually taken control of the home.

This family was practically being held hostage by a little terror of a toy poodle who would bark frantically each time the widowed mother and her teenage daughter tried to speak to each other. Complicating the picture was another daughter, who didn't get along with her sister.

His "high-pitched, whining bark" when they ate was so obnoxious, the women had actually stopped eating at home and ate all their meals out at restaurants to avoid dealing with his disruption! To get any peace from his pestering when they were home, the women used to lock themselves in their rooms – though he'd continue to stand guard and yap outside the door.

Through careful questioning and observation, Dr. Tortora finally determined something that shocked his clients more than their dog's outrageous bullying behavior: They were unconsciously and unknowingly rewarding this tiny tyrant by giving in to him.

This "dumb animal" knew exactly how to manipulate this already neurotic household so that he could get just what he wanted (he even "ganged-up" on the teenager by jumping on her, just as the mother and other daughter picked on her) – driving them all nuts in the process.

PINPOINT THE PROBLEM

The first step is to be able to describe to your veterinarian what exactly is the behavior problem. To do this, you need to carefully observe the pet and determine when, where, how often, with whom, and what it is that she does that is causing the difficulty.

Try keeping a chart if necessary, especially if you aren't around all day and there are other caretakers involved. Is this a consistent problem? Is kitty "spending a penny" in everyone's shoes, or only your new boyfriend's Italian loafers? Has she always acted this weird way, in which case the problem may simply be bad breeding, or is this a new twist?

Why does a previously pleasant pet suddenly turn into the devil cat from Hades? One often overlooked problem is physical illness. A cat with a urinary tract infection will be unable to control herself, and seemingly "forget" to use the litter box.

Any sudden change in trained behaviors should be a clear signal to call the veterinarian and make an appointment. The problem may be an easily treatable infection, irritation or allergy; or as serious as a brain lesion or case of epilepsy. The first thing to do is rule out any physiological reason for the change in behavior.

The next step is to be able to describe to your veterinarian what exactly is the behavior problem. From your chart, you may see clues in the timing, frequency or location where the behavior has seemingly become "unlearned" or forgotten.

Especially since we're talking here about a previously trained pet appearing to unlearn her training, consider what is new or different about your household or situation since just before the offensive behavior began.

Is there a new baby or family member? Have you changed the brand of kitty litter in the cat box? Rearranged the furniture or the pet's sleeping or feeding area? Did Grandpa just come to live with you? Did you adopt a stray? Are there strays hanging about outside?

The issues in these cases could be territorial, particularly if problems with elimination behavior are involved. A new cat introduced to a household that has a long-time pet in residence triggers dominance and territorial issues.

If you freak out when kitty enters the baby's room because you believe that cats want to sneak into a baby's crib to suck its breath and suffocate it, you will unknowingly be teaching kitty by your attitude and actions to fear or mistrust the baby. Kitty may associate the screaming or chasing away or spanking with being near the baby and will either fear the infant or act aggressively toward it at some point.

UNTIL CAT DO US PART

Some pets that suddenly turn nervous or frightened or aggressive may be mirroring chaotic emotions in the home. Even the most amicable of divorces and remarriages are upsetting to us humans, and animals pick up this insecurity from us.

Dominance and territory may also be interwoven issues here as well, particularly if a beloved mistress suddenly has a new man in her heart and in her bed — even more so if the cat used to share this bed, and is now locked out of the bedroom.

By the way, if your cat really seems to dislike your latest date or mate-to-be, it may be wise to have second thoughts. Even people who won't admit to believing in ESP agree that an animal's instinctual responses to people are very often right on the money.

Through careful sleuthing and analyzing of the before-and-after behavior patterns, you may be able to unravel the puzzle of your disturbed pet yourself. If you can't, or if uncovering the reason still leaves you stymied as to how to solve it, consider asking your vet about a referral to an animal behaviorist.

Sometimes the behavior is so aggressive that action must be taken as soon as possible — especially if there are children involved. Sometimes there is no other recourse than to find a new home for the animal or, in extreme cases when all else fails, to put the animal to sleep.

GROOMING, FLEAS AND MORE

Good grooming as well as good food is essential for optimum health and for sheer aesthetic beauty. Grooming your cat is also a nice way to enhance the lines of communication between you and your pet. Believe it or not, a simple stroking or petting counts as good grooming. By stroking your cat, you are distributing natural body oils throughout her skin and giving her a nice, shiny coat.

Kitty will also thank you for your mini-massage with a peaceful purr! Cats love to be stroked and petted and will often reward you with a satisfied "Meow!"

"She is feeling well, because her eyes are clear and her coat is smooth..."
– Frances and Richard Lockridge

To help keep your cat's coat shiny, brush her daily with a good brush made specially for cat's fur. Keep the strokes firm and long, to help remove entrenched hair. Sure, cats keep themselves very clean by licking, but if she is shedding excessively, she may be licking up too much hair and in turn, swallowing it to create dangerous hairballs. Hairballs cause a host of respiratory and digestive disorders.

Daily brushing helps remove excess hair. You can also brush a little cornstarch into her hair to keep it clean. Professional groomers add some lemon juice mixed with water to make light-haired cats' coats shine.

Let the lemon juice sit on her coat just before bath-time. Yes, cats can and should be bathed! Although most cat owners balk at the idea of putting a screaming, clawing cat into a tub of soapy water, if you do it right you won't have a fuss on your hands.

First, get the cat used to the tub. Let her sit and simply play in whatever receptacle you'll be using as a bathtub. Add a few of her favorite toys for good measure. Next, add a little warm water. Tell her that it's okay and splash her playfully without frightening her.

Show kitty the spray attachment to your faucet. Let her play with it, but don't turn it on! When kitty is perfectly comfortable with her bath area, it's time to give her her first good soaking. Hopefully, you haven't waited until kitty is a senior citizen to do this! The younger you teach your cat how wonderful bath-time can be, the better.

Put some cotton balls moistened with a little mineral oil into your cat's ears. This will protect the ears from water entering into the canal. Use a mild cat shampoo – not one made for humans! There are plenty on the market, available in pet or health food stores. Check with your vet to see if he or she recommends a specific shampoo for your breed of cat.

NO SNIFFLES!

Wash your cat on a warm day and not too close to bedtime. You don't want kitty to catch the sniffles!

Wet the hair down thoroughly and apply the shampoo, gently massaging all the while. By now, kitty may have even relaxed enough to enjoy her bath! If the directions on the shampoo say to leave it on for a while – especially important with an anti-flea shampoo or one for dry hair – amuse your cat as much as you can so that she doesn't become bored and try to flee.

Now rinse very carefully, trying to avoid the eye area. Get ALL the soap out of kitty's fur. Always towel dry your cat immediately after a bath. If you can get her to stand still long enough to use the blow-dryer on her fur, all the better.

Brush her down after you finish drying. *Voila!* Now you have a squeaky clean kitty!

Keep kitty's nails clipped regularly. Nail clipping is easy, and once kitty gets used to the process, she'll actually look forward to her manicure. Cats do not like to have excessively long nails and will try to pull off the too long nail in desperation with their teeth.

To clip a cat's nails, hold her gently in your lap using soothing words and stroking her fur gently. Using a good quality nail clipper, snip off ONLY THE ENDS. Don't try to take off too much. You may cut into the "quick" of her nail and cause bleeding.

One trick I've learned after clipping hundreds of claws is to work speedily and confidently. If you show that you're nervous – and who isn't the first time they tackle a cat manicure! – your cat will pick up your insecurity and become fearful.

Clean the ears with a piece of cotton ball dipped in a little mineral oil. If a cat's ears smell badly, do check with your vet. Foul odors may signal ear infections that should be treated professionally.

Fleas can be a problem in many states. Stay one step ahead of these pests by inspecting kitty frequently for fleas (and ticks). Use a flea comb to remove the little suckers. You may have to resort to one of the variety of flea treatments available in supermarkets and pet specialty stores if your flea problem persists.

You'll also have to tackle your home environment once fleas have made their entry. Good old-fashioned borax (available at your supermarket in the laundry aid section) sprinkled on carpets and floors is one safe way to destroy fleas and their eggs. If this natural remedy doesn't work, you may have to resort to professional help to rid your home of fleas.

Generally speaking, if you keep your cat indoors or in your immediate environment (a treated backyard), you should not have a flea problem. We've lived in Florida, a state notorious for its fleas, for eight years with four animals and haven't seen hide nor hair of a flea on our pets. Maybe it's because I recite nightly prayers to the Flea God to stay away, but more likely it is because we keep a close and meticulous watch on our animals to head off a potential problem before it begins.

On a personal note, although it may sound antisocial, I do not permit four-footed visitors to my home unless I know both pet and owner well. It takes just one flea to start a whole population of insects that will keep you scratching for dear life. I don't need this problem nor do my pets. Although this policy has caused hard feelings with some individuals, it's my policy.

I also do not pet other people's cats when I visit for the same reason. I can admire them from a distance but I do not have to touch them. I once lost a very precious Siamese by ignoring this policy and allowing a friend to bring his cat over for a visit. The cat, recently brought home from the Humane Society, had had all his shots but apparently was carrying the distemper virus on its skin. The virus killed one of my kittens and almost killed Bobby, who was a baby at the time. Fortunately, a kindly vet and a week of blood transfusions saved his life. This experience only reinforces that a somewhat selfish attitude protects your pets from harm.

BEHAVIORAL PROBLEMS

Every now and then a cat owner will develop a special problem with his or her pet. Usually this takes the form of a cat scratching, biting or otherwise destroying personal property or going potty in inappropriate areas!

Let's backtrack a moment. In order to help prevent behavioral problems, it is essential to choose your cat wisely. Selecting a healthy, well-bred kitten is an important key to preventing future problems. You can save a life by picking up a pet at the local Humane Society or adopting a stray from a local shelter. However, do your homework if you are looking for a purebred. There are many unscrupulous breeders out there who breed cats in a factory-like atmosphere. These "kitty mills" produce litters of pets purely for profit and do not take the necessary time to help the mother cat spend those important few weeks with her kittens, teaching them good grooming habits and getting them familiar with their surroundings.

One of the first signs of a poor breeder, in my mind, is the odor of the cattery. I trust my nose to tell me if the breeder is overburdened with cats and cannot keep their living area clean. Foul odors also spell poor hygiene. Chances are that a cat coming out of such an environment will not develop good personal habits. She may not use her litter box properly and begin to soil your furniture or go potty in your precious plants.

SCREEN BREEDERS

Cats from poor breeders may also inherit diseases or congenital illnesses that will show up as she ages. I had one hapless Siamese from such a breeder who was so poorly bred and socialized, she was a sheer terror to have in the house. Cleopatra was so fearful that it was an almost impossible task for her to feel comfortable around humans and all our other pets.

She also had a terrible eye problem which required daily medication. It was a nightmare trying to catch and pin her down to administer her medication! And this task only served to make her more fearful.

Finally, we had to give her up to a kindly veterinarian who agreed to care for her in his hospital. He kept her in a clean cage and at night let her roam freely. One of the nurses took a shine to Cleo and began taking her home for visits. Eventually, after months of tender loving care and gradual resocialization, Cleo came around. The last I heard she was doing very well. Her eyes are perfect and she is now living full time at the nurse's home.

Not every story has such a happy ending. I have met dozens of cat owners who grew to detest their pet because of a seemingly unbreakable habit and gave it up to the pound – an unfortunate solution to a potentially solvable problem.

I learned from Cleo's experience that almost every cat can be helped through her trauma with loving observation and patience.

Many experts believe that boredom is at the root of a great many bad habits. A bored cat will deliberately seek out mischief. That is why it is especially important to keep your cat active or get her a companion.

If your cat is destructive and your home is beginning to look like a war zone, it is time to take action.

Remember that cats instinctively claw and scratch. It is their nature. You should have at least one or preferably two scratching posts around the house to keep kitty occupied and happy. I prefer the plain old-fashioned – and cheap! – scratching posts that are simply wooden posts covered with tough, industrial carpeting. I've had one for 10 years now and it is still going strong!

You can use a plain old log as a scratching area, too. When kitty heads for the furniture, gently but firmly say, "No!" and redirect it toward the scratching post. If this does not work, you may have to resort to the watergun technique. I don't like to use this myself, but it works. Simply spray kitty with a shot of water (don't be cruel and drench the cat, however!) and she will surely leave the scene of the crime!

Also make sure that her claws are well trimmed. Long nails are very uncomfortable for cats and they will do anything to alleviate the discomfort. DO NOT DE-CLAW CATS! It is a cruel and unnecessary procedure, similar to cutting your own fingers off at the knuckles.

HOT PEPPERS

Some people advise putting Tabasco sauce or hot pepper sauce around the area your cat is destroying, but this is not needed if you firmly and consistently show kitty the scratching post.

Be sure, too, that kitty has a bundle of play toys to amuse her. Housebound cats need that extra stimulation.

Rotate the toys so that your cat doesn't become bored with the same selection. It's much like the tactics you use with young children: distract, distract, distract! Soon kitty will forget about tearing apart your good couch and concentrate on her own toys.

There are certain commercial products that deter scratching and chewing. You can place these ill-tasting (to cats) products anywhere kitty tends to claw or bite. The only problem with some of them is they smell so badly, they keep humans at bay as well!

Warren Eckstein offers a most unusual tip for pesky cats: Tie blown-up balloons to the sides of chairs, walls or sofas, wherever kitty is scratching. If kitty leaps onto one of the balloons, it will naturally break, giving kitty quite a loud and meaningful correction.

Aluminum foil, too, acts as a deterrent. Place foil around the problem areas. Cats hate the feel of foil when they walk on it and will stay clear of these areas. Another trick is a "shaker can." Fill an empty soda can with a few pennies, enough to make a loud noise when you rattle the can. Tie the can to the end of the sofa or place it on the counter if kitty has a tendency to steal food. When kitty leaps up and tips over the can, the loud rattle will scare the dickens out of her!

If kitty has developed the bad habit of using your plants as litter boxes or chewing the leaves, try any of the above techniques to discourage this practice. Also, be sure that the cat's own litter box is kept scrupulously clean. Never use one litter box for more than two cats. Clean out the box daily to remove fecal matter and change the litter twice weekly.

There is a relatively new type of litter on the market that claims to last almost forever. The ads say that you never have to change the litter box again. Urine clings to the litter and forms clumps that can be removed and flushed down the toilet. When the litter gradually decreases, you simply add more.

I've tried this litter and have not found it satisfactory for a two-cat home. In a short time the urine sinks to the bottom of the box and odors develop. My vet isn't overly fond of the product either because he feels bacteria will eventually grow in the litter. It's also quite costly. You are better off, in my opinion, buying the cheapest litter available and changing the litter box often. A colleague of mine who houses eight cats uses shredded, unprinted newsprint because it is cheap and works well. She simply takes out the newspaper each day and provides fresh "litter" for her happy cats. And her house never smells like a cattery!

Speaking of litter boxes, I also prefer the large, hooded kind. One of my litter boxes has a charcoal filter built into its hood that is replaceable. The charcoal absorbs odors. I feel that cats, being fastidious and private little beasties, like to have a covered toilet.

NEUTERING

Aggressive cats may be calmed by either spaying or neutering – a good idea for all cats since we have such a tremendous overpopulation of felines in this country.

If your cat starts biting your ankles or otherwise harassing you, redirect her aggression to one of her swinging toys. Let her know with a firm voice command that this is not acceptable behavior. Don't get into the habit of "roughhousing" with your cat. She'll think you accept this behavior. Treat your cat gently and she will develop kinder and gentler habits.

Some cats develop the habit of chewing wool. This usually occurs in Siamese or Burmese cats with greater frequency than in other breeds. Generally, only kittens will chew wool and, if discouraged, will grow out of the habit. Make sure that your little chewer is getting a healthy diet and that she has lots of kitty toys to play with and chew instead of your good sweater. Sometimes dabbing a bit of cologne on the object of her affection will help deter your cat's chewing. Cats detest the smell of perfume!

Remember that punishment is only effective if you catch your cat in the act – which is very rare in catdom! You are far better off preventing and deterring bad behavior with intelligence and a loving hand. Don't forget your communication skills. If kitty is up to no good, send her a mental message and give her a firm verbal "No!" and she will get the message.

Remember, too, that cats do undergo periods of stress. I know that both of mine react horrendously to change. When we have houseguests, both Bobby and Brutus seem to be on their worst behavior. Brutus, especially, becomes so unnerved by an extra body or two floating around that he often becomes physically ill. Try to keep a consistent household and a general feeling of calm in your home to ensure well-adjusted cats.

ON THE MOVE

If you are moving or traveling with kitty, use every means in your power to make the transition smooth. I've heard of many cases where cats moved to a new location become so upset that they make the arduous journey back to their original residence – even if it is hundreds of miles away!

For this reason, it is much better to keep a watchful eye on your cat when you are in transit and keep her confined to a large crate or cage. When you arrive at your destination, confine the cat to one room until she adjusts to the new scenario. Gradually introduce her to other areas of the house. We have found that the best way to orientate Bobby and Brutus is to confine them to a bathroom area (toilet seat down, please!) with their litter and a bowl of water provided.

After awhile, we bring them into the kitchen area for a meal. Within several hours, they're happy as cats can be, busily exploring their new territory.

While we are on the subject of moving, you may find that traveling with your cat can be heaven or hell. There are some cats who naturally take to automobile travel, but the majority of cats hate being in a moving object.

Get your cat accustomed to car travel by taking short rides – not only to the vet, please! – so that your kitty gets used to the ride. Make the ride as pleasant as possible. Speak softly to the cat and let her know how much you love her.

Of course, there are exceptional cats who will never get used to car travel and complain throughout the journey. We have a 12-hour drive to our country home and Bobby, the first time out, yowled constantly along the way. It was an absolute nightmare that almost brought my husband and me to blows! That Siamese yowl can be most unnerving.

The next trip, acting upon the advice of our vet, we gave him a mild tranquilizer. He was mellow and fine during the entire journey. Another problem solved!

If you cannot take your cat with you during your vacation, the best solution is to have someone come into the house and care for your cat, even if he or she comes in only once daily. Ask your vet for a recommendation.

Cats do not generally fare well in boarding kennels since they truly prefer their own environment, but if you must board them, visit the premises prior to boarding to make sure that the facility is clean and comfortable and that there is a vet on board in case something goes awry in your absence.

Flying is another possibility if you want to vacation with your cat. Some airlines permit you to keep your pet underneath your seat in an approved pet carrier. Larger cats will have to go into the cargo section. Again, please call your favorite airline to check out their pet policies. There is a charge for handling, of course, and your pet must be enclosed in a specially designed and airline-approved carrier. You can include your cat's favorite toy or blanket if she feels more secure about having a familiar object with her. You will also be asked to produce a recent note from your vet guaranteeing that all kitty's shots are up-to-date. Traveling across borders is even more complicated. Your cat may have to be quarantined for a period of time.

CHECK PERSONALLY

On a personal note: Make sure that if you are flying with a pet you watch the cargo being loaded onto the plane. We were traveling with a puppy a few years ago and were aghast when we noticed that the luggage carriers did not load our kennel into the hatch. As much as we fussed and complained, the personnel of that airline (I won't mention names even though it kills me!) lent a most unsympathetic ear to our plight. I was in tears as I begged the attendant to track our little beagle down. Finally, after delaying the plane's departure by a full half hour, they located the puppy and put him on board. I shudder even thinking what could have happened if we hadn't been so diligent! He could have ended up in Alaska for all we know!

Once you arrive at your destination, you'll find that not a great many hotels allow pets in the rooms. There are hotel chains that do accept pets, however. Do take the time to phone ahead and check out which chains do or do not allow pets. And if you will be in the room for several days, make sure that you tell the maid or desk clerk not to open the door to your room under any circumstances! Place a warning sign on the door as well. Clean up your own room or take the pet out when the maid cleans. You don't want to ruin your vacation looking for a runaway pet.

As a safety precaution, make sure that kitty is wearing her collar and I.D. tag. Most pet stores and vets sell these little plaques on which you inscribe the pet's name, your name, address and telephone number and any other pertinent information that would be helpful – God forbid – if kitty escaped!

If all this seems rather overwhelming, don't get bogged down with the details. Problems with cats rarely occur if you keep the lines of communication open, feed and care for them lovingly, and pay attention to the medical requirements necessary to protect your cat from disease.

CATS AND CLAIRVOYANCE

"**C**ats possess so many mysterious abilities, they are uncanny," says experimental psychologist David Greene, who has spent 10 years studying the mind of the cat. "Whether it's an alley cat or a prize-winning Persian, any cat can perform absolutely astonishing mental, physical and extrasensory feats."

Dr. Michael Fox, scientific director of the U.S. Humane Society in Washington, D.C., has collected hundreds of examples of the astonishing ability of cats to read the moods and feelings of their owners. And there are volumes of evidence that cats possess remarkable powers.

Greene uses cats in the treatment and rehabilitation of the mentally ill in hospitals in England. During his research, he has chronicled remarkable cat case histories which, he says, include:

- Predicting natural disasters before they happen;
- Saving people and animals from death or injury;
- Tracking owners over incredible distances; and
- Carrying out complex tasks with superhuman intellect.

In his book *Your Incredible Cats* (Doubleday), Greene highlights the case of the cat that saved a baby. He writes that Virgil McMillan of Berryville, Arkansas, found a starving kitten, nursed it back to health and named it Slowly.

For two years, Slowly went out for a nightly prowl but always returned home within an hour. One freezing night, however, he didn't return, and Virgil and his wife searched vainly for him for half the night.

In the morning, Virgil went looking for the cat again. While searching through an old barn, he found a sack. When he moved it to one side, the cat wriggled out, looked at him and then crawled back inside the sack. Virgil opened the sack and to his astonishment, found Slowly licking a half-naked baby boy. The baby was close to death and doctors said that only the heat from the cat's body had kept the child alive throughout the night.

Says Greene: "No one could explain how Slowly knew a baby had been abandoned in that sack. Experts said the ice-hard ground would have made it difficult for the cat to pick up any scent. What sense took the cat there we'll never know, but he somehow knew that the child's life depended on him."

"There are many cases of cats saving families by giving early warnings of quakes," he says. "But they can also foresee small-scale accidents in the home."

The uncanny vibes of one ginger tomcat called Barney saved an entire family from injury, recalls Greene. The cat loved to snooze on top of the TV, but one night, while the family was watching a program, he suddenly jumped down and glared at the screen.

Greene also says cats can predict earthquakes and volcanic eruptions 48 hours before they happen. Scientists monitoring earth tremors in California say cats can sense them long before the most delicate of man's instruments.

Then he leapt for the door, screeching frantically, indicating they should follow him. Seconds later, the TV set exploded.

"If Barney had stayed, he would have been badly hurt and so might the family," says Greene. "His uncanny senses warned him something dreadful was about to happen."

In his investigations, Greene came across many remarkable demonstrations of cats' clairvoyance and telepathy.

One cat called Fidget was locked up in a house with food while his master went on a one-day business trip. On the way home, the man was injured in a traffic accident and two days later, he died. A sympathetic local policeman fed the cat while relatives decided what to do with him.

Somehow, Fidget knew his owner had passed away. When mourners turned up for the funeral miles from the house, they found the cat sitting by the open grave.

"The cat sat motionless until the coffin was lowered," says Greene. "Then he turned and walked away with the mourners watching. How he knew where and when his friend would be buried, in a large graveyard miles away from his home, is beyond human comprehension."

BAFFLED

Another recorded case still baffles Greene.

This one involved a Siamese called Fingal who would tap on the window of his owner's home at exactly nine o'clock every night to get in after his evening walk. When he died, incredibly, the tapping continued! Months later a friend of Celia Dale, his mistress, brought her own pet cat to the house. It started to walk toward what had been Fingal's favorite armchair when suddenly it froze in its tracks, arched its back and spat in rage.

"It was exactly as if she could see another cat on the chair," says Celia. "So at the time Fingal normally went out for the evening, I opened the window and the visiting cat relaxed."

Says researcher Greene: "It was as though the cat had seen the ghost of another cat leaving the room. Miss Dale could never explain that tapping, but she always opened the window when she heard it and the noise stopped. Was she letting the ghost of Fingal in just as she had let him in during his lifetime? I can't answer that. Cats have quite incredible powers, but we still have a long, long way to go to understand them."

Cats really do seem to be in tune with the occult and possess amazing psychic powers that are far beyond those of humans or other pets, say animal experts.

"Cats are more aware of apparitions, ghosts and spiritual bodies, while dogs' psychic powers are more focused on their masters," said Bill Schul, a Winfield, Kansas, psychologist.

"GHOST" CATS

Some pets are so devoted to people that there are reports of them even "returning from the dead" to help their masters in a crisis. Schul says there are countless reports of families being awakened by the mewing of the family pet and finding that the house is on fire — when their pet had died months or even years before.

By watching the body language of our pets, we can tune in to their psychic wavelengths.

"The animal assumes he's communicating with us through his psychic cues. And by watching him closely, we can see these cues and become even closer to our pets," Schul explained.

Cats, for example, are aware of the presence of out-of-body spirits, and may react in a friendly or frightened manner, depending on what kind of spirit they are dealing with, says Schul. People don't want to believe that animals have extra sensory perception, he says, because they like to think that only humans have it.

SULKY

Pets know when their masters are leaving on a trip or about to come home, he says, usually sulking for days in advance – and perking up days before the return.

And although many people – usually those who don't love cats – think cats are aloof and indifferent creatures, they are actually well aware of their masters' sicknesses and deaths, even over great distances.

Researcher Joseph Wylder of Stockbridge, Massachusetts, says he has heard of pets traveling hundreds of miles to find their owner who is in the hospital.

Says Wylder, "There is a lot more to pets than I thought. But you must open up to your pet and have respect for it. Pets can communicate in ways we have yet to appreciate."

To tune in to your cat and its psychic powers, Schul and Wylder suggest the following:

❖ Be very quiet in the cat's presence. Attune yourself to the cat by putting yourself in her place.

❖ Watch her body language signals and you'll be able to sense your cat's thoughts. If you don't try to tune in to this, your pet will grow away from you emotionally.

91

❖ Try to send your pet mental pictures and watch how she responds.

"Your cat doesn't understand why we have to turn the light on in the dark, so you must let her know what you are thinking through the mental telepathy you send to her," said Schul.

One of America's leading psychics is convinced that the cat has psychic powers that foretell the future, bring luck, or can even put a death whammy on you!

"Next to human beings, cats have the most potential to develop and use psychic powers," says David Guardino, the Las Vegas-based psychic to the stars.

"This is why cats have always been associated with witches. People who have occult powers know that cats can help them increase these powers.

"My own research has shown me that cats even have the power to destroy people. It's very bad luck to kill or injure a cat. I know of many people who have died or encountered serious misfortune after doing so."

PSYCHIC

Guardino says cats quite definitely have the ability to see into the future. He says he has heard of cats that acted very strangely just before their owners died.

"In one instance, an old lady was in the hospital and her daughter was looking after her cat," Guardino says. "The cat behaved fine until one night when it started to act up. It ran screeching through the house, inconsolable. A few minutes later the daughter got a call that her mother had passed away."

Guardino thinks that cats can bring you good luck or bad luck depending on whether they like or dislike you.

"A lot of successful gamblers have pet cats because they believe that. They make sure to treat them well, so that they get good luck when they are gambling."

Guardino also believes that cats can warn people of impending disasters. Often, he says, owners are awakened by their cat because something is wrong – something potentially disastrous. And he insists that cats can actually sense the presence of people who have died – "gone over to the other side," as he puts it.

DEPARTED SPIRITS

"Cats do have the ability to sense departed spirits. Often, they sense the presence of ghosts even when others see nothing. I have seen cats whose owner had died go toward something invisible, then rub themselves against an invisible leg just like they did to their deceased owner when he was alive.

"They have amazing powers. I have known cats to foretell the birth of babies. In one case, a cat became very agitated in front of its owner who was pregnant. She didn't feel anything and the baby was not due, but a few hours later she was rushed to hospital and had a premature delivery."

Guardino said that alley cats will often use a kind of psychic power to avoid being picked up as strays. "Alley cats have psychic radar that makes them too smart to get picked up. They have the ability to sense when people are after them, just like the big cats in the jungle."

INCREDIBLE JOURNEYS

One area of interest to researchers is the cat's uncanny ability to travel enormous distances over totally unknown territory to reach a particular destination. It's known to scientists as "psi-trailing," and there are countless stories of cats journeying hundreds of miles to track down an owner or return to an old home. For example:

❖ An army sergeant in Kokomo, Indiana, took his yellow tomcat, Corporal, with him when he was transferred to a base near Augusta, Georgia. The cat apparently decided that it didn't care for the Deep South – and made the 700-mile journey back to his old home in only three weeks. He couldn't have remembered the route because he had made the trip down to Georgia in a closed box – on board an express train!

❖ Rusty walked an arduous 16 miles over unknown territory to find his way back home. The astonishing journey began shortly after his owners, Geoffrey and Sandra Langrish of Camberley, England, discovered they were expecting a baby. Thinking the cat might be jealous, they decided it would be best to give him away.

Rhoda Young, who lived in the next town, offered to take him in. Geoffrey and Sandra put Rusty in a basket and drove him to his new home.

When they reached Mrs. Young's home 16 miles away, the feisty puss shot out of the basket as soon as it was opened – and vanished. Seven months later, plump and healthy and very standoffish, he popped through his special opening in the door of the Langrish kitchen.

Where had he been for these seven long months? Living wild? He seemed to be in much too good shape for that. Boarding with some cat lovers somewhere between the two homes? Well, of course Rusty wasn't telling – and even local animal experts were dumbfounded that he had found his way over a route that he had traveled only once before, virtually blindfolded!

Geoffrey and Sandra were so touched by his devotion, they decided to keep him. But his experience seems to have given Rusty a touch of wanderlust and he disappears from time to time, always returning. And at the time of this writing, he is off on his travels again. The Langrish family patiently awaits his return!

❄ Farmer Alfonse Mondry's cat, Misele, couldn't stand it when her 82-year-old master was taken to a hospital in Sarrebourg, France. Some incredible homing instinct sent Misele heading straight for her master nine miles cross country – through stone quarries, fields, forests and busy highways. At the hospital, where she had never been before, she sneaked past orderlies and found old Alfonse's room. She pushed the door open and jumped onto his bed. When nurses and doctors found the cat purring contentedly across their patient's legs, they didn't have the heart to separate them.

❄ Princess, a gorgeous calico cat that was a pampered house pet, had only been outdoors twice in her life when she got lost on a trip. The bereft Keaton family, of Grand Rapids, Michigan, was sure she would perish. But the astonishing Princess turned up three days later. And – amazingly – she had covered 100 miles in that time!

The three-year-old cat's bewildering odyssey began after Ronald Keaton and his six-year-old daughter Stacy climbed into their van with the family dog and Princess to drive from their home in Grand Rapids to Toledo, Ohio.

Mrs. Keaton, Peggy, and their other two children, Ronnie, 4, and Meagan, 2, had already gone ahead to Toledo to be with Mrs. Keaton's ailing mother.

The family said Princess's long journey started when Stacy and her Dad stopped at a highway rest area 100 miles from home.

"They made a pit stop in Brighton and the cat was certainly still in the van then," says Peggy Keaton. "My husband remembers he had trouble getting in because Princess was against the window on the driver's side.

"Stacy got in on the passenger side and lifted the cat out of the way. They thought she went into the back of the van and they didn't stop until they reached Toledo. It was only then they discovered she was missing."

Three nights later, a neighbor spotted Princess on the doorstep of the Keatons' house in Grand Rapids. "She jumped up on her favorite window sill and the neighbors telephoned us," Mrs. Keaton said. But when the Keatons returned home, Princess did not give them a warm welcome. "She was mad with Ronnie," says Peggy Keaton. "She hissed at him."

❧ Sugar was a cream-colored semi-Persian that lived with the Smith family in Anderson, California. When the family decided to move back to Oklahoma, they wanted to take the cat with them, but left her behind because she was so terrified of cars. So Sugar was left with a kindly neighbor who agreed to take her in.

Fourteen months later, in Oklahoma, a cream-colored, semi-Persian leaped on Mrs. Smith's shoulder while she was working in the garden. She thought the cat looked like her Sugar but she couldn't believe it, even though a stray cat – or any cat for that matter – is unlikely to leap onto the shoulder of a stranger.

But her doubts vanished completely when she felt the deformed bone on the cat's left hip joint – one of Sugar's unique physical characteristics.

She called the neighbor back in Anderson and was told that, sure enough, Sugar had disappeared after only two weeks in her adoptive home. The astonishing cat had tracked the family she loved over desert, mountain and bustling highways more than 1,500 miles!

❧ In 1977, when the Hicks family was about to leave home in Adelaide, Australia, on a long trip overseas, 15-year-old Kirsten asked her grandparents – who lived 1,000 miles from Adelaide – to look after her Persian, Howie. They agreed, but when Kirsten returned from abroad she was heartbroken to learn that Howie had vanished and every effort to trace him had failed.

Almost a year later, a bedraggled cat appeared at the Hicks' home. It was matted, filthy and bleeding. At first the Hicks weren't sure who it was – although Kirsten recognized her cat instantly. And the once-gorgeous house pet purred happily when she picked him up in her arms and cuddled him.

Howie's journey had taken 12 months. He had crossed wild rivers and fought his way across the deserts and wilderness of the Australian outback. How did that pampered puss do it? It goes to show, say experts, who are as dumbfounded as any of us, that underneath the sleepy exterior of the pampered house pet is a remarkable creature of astonishing courage and resilience.